Praise for Lee Hillberg

"Although I have not known Lee for very long, I have seen him escalate from a spiritual introduction to a full-fledged practitioner. Anyone that knows Lee knows he does nothing halfway—it's not only all or nothing, it will also be the best.

"His book takes him from his initial introduction to spiritualism by his beloved grandmother when he was a child to his present day as a recognized, practicing healer.

"Those that study and know spirituality know one is not given healing gifts until they heal themselves . . . A true healer is not allowed to skip this step. Lee has worked on self-healing all his life.

"His book is fascinating in his description of his progress with connecting with the universe and trusting the information. Another law: you don't truly connect unless you trust. The universe chooses healers very carefully and healers use different modalities to heal. I congratulate Lee and thank him for being a healer with colors!

"I am proud to call Lee friend and colleague."

—Carolyn Cummings

"Writing this book has been a multiyear undertaking, a driven and unwavering devotion to capture what he has learned and to share it with others. I am immensely proud of Lee for this accomplishment. How many people feel they have something to share, feel they have a book 'in them' and never pursue it? Too many to count. My heart is filled with pride and admiration for Lee; he followed his heart and his calling. Let us all follow his example."

—A. S. Hill

"This is a beautiful story of a man's pursuit of connection with Spirit for the benefit of others.

"Just as people speak many different languages and dialects, so the Creator speaks to each of us in the language we understand best. The trick is to listen and you can develop that ability as you would a muscle—with practice and repetition.

"Spirit led Lee to the expression and ritual that spoke to his heart, and this book can be an invaluable tool for you, too, to develop and think about your own.

"Create your own sacred space. Fill it with objects that are meaningful for you and that draw you closer to your own understanding of healing and spiritual development. Have fun! Be childlike and open to wonder. Believe it and you will see it!

"I wish you joy, love, peace, and health."

—Trish Gurney
Emei Qi Gong Master

One Man's Spiritual Journey to
Healing with Color Energy

One Man's Spiritual Journey to
Healing with Color Energy

Lee Hillberg

Mountain Arbor
PRESS
Alpharetta, GA

This book is not intended as a substitute for the medical advice of physicians. The reader should consult a physician regularly in any matters relating to his/her health, particularly with respect to any symptoms or illness that may require diagnosis or medical attention.

Copyright © 2017 by Lee Hillberg

All rights reserved. No part of this book may be reproduced or transmitted in any form or by any means, electronic or mechanical, including photocopying, recording, or any information storage and retrieval system, without permission in writing from the author.

ISBN: 978-1-63183-064-8

This ISBN is the property of Mountain Arbor Press for the express purpose of sales and distribution of this title. The content of this book is the property of the copyright holder only. Mountain Arbor Press does not hold any ownership of the content of this book and is not liable in any way for the materials contained within. The views and opinions expressed in this book are the property of the Author/Copyright holder, and do not necessarily reflect those of Mountain Arbor Press.

Library of Congress Control Number: 2016920896

10 9 8 7 6 5 4 3 2   022717

Printed in the United States of America

∞This paper meets the requirements of ANSI/NISO Z39.48-1992 (Permanence of Paper)

To Mother and Billie, both pillars of strength and unconditional love.

Contents

Foreword	ix
Acknowledgments	xi
What Is Spiritual Healing?	xiii

Part I

1.	The Early Years	3
2.	Storm Clouds: Depression, Drought, and Hope	13
3.	The Military	25
4.	The Business Years	29

Part II

5.	Transition to Spirituality	41
6.	Native Americans	47
7.	Initiation	59
8.	It's Time	77
9.	The Power of Color	81
10.	Nature's Magic	101
11.	Carter Shepard	117
12.	Healings	129
13.	Lessons from Spirit	143
14.	Connecting with Spirit	159

Learnings	177
Special Messages	189
Bibliography	193

Foreword

Every now and then, someone steps into your life and changes it forever. Your whole perspective of the world changes because this person gave you a new way of looking at it. You begin to notice that the sun shines a little brighter and the rain soothes and refreshes the soul just a little more than it did before they came along.

My cousin Billie introduced me to Lee several years ago. He immediately became family and a friend. He taught me to be compassionate and forgiving to others as well as to myself. I never realized that I was limiting the power of love and forgiveness by neglecting to apply it to my own life and transgressions.

Lee shared his gift of healing with me when I became afflicted with headaches and depression. The color blue has proven to be the remedy for most of my headaches, while orange aids in my chronic depression. He has performed shamanic healing prayers and applied color to heal a medically diagnosed tumor in my breast.

In this society, pain and suffering abound. It seems we have lost touch with the natural, not to mention miraculous, works of God. We forget to look to Him for our needs. So many neglect the healing power of nature that our Creator so abundantly provides. Lee reminds us of the presence and power of God and Spirit. He reminds us that we have alternatives. We can choose to take an active role in our health and well-being. We can live the life God intended and enjoy the incredible gift of nature.

In this book, Lee tells us about his life and spiritual walk. His keen understanding of nature and the contribution it makes in our lives is astounding. He ensures that the reader understands the effect and use of color to aid in the healing process.

I have experienced, firsthand, the commitment and passion Lee has for his mission. He welcomes the opportunity to spread God's healing and love to any who ask. It is a calling and Lee never fails to answer. He is a true shaman, medicine man, and healer.

—Laura Knight

Acknowledgments

I have been blessed in this journey to have so many wonderful people come into my life at just the right time. This includes relatives, friends, extended family, and my many helpers from the other side, i.e., teachers, guides, family, and angels, to name some. You have all helped and supported my growth and progress. I have always said there were angels in my path.

A very special thanks to Billie. Without her, there would not have been a book. She has been a physical-world guide who has taught me unconditional love.

Thank you, Carolyn. My time with you has been life altering. To my friend Trish Gurney for using her postsurgical recovery time to proofread. Laura Knight, who spent many hours editing and transcribing.

To all, please accept my love and gratitude for being part of my Journey.

What Is Spiritual Healing?

A spiritual healer is one who is an open channel for the flow of energy and healing light.

The source of all healing comes from God.

Anyone can become a spiritual healer. We are all spiritual. As long as one's intentions are to promote and channel God's healings, one can become a healer.

Utilizing spirit guides, color, auras, the chakras, and even totems, spiritual healing can and does work in full harmony with traditional medicine.

Prayer and meditation work hand in hand with spiritual healing. Prayer is us talking to God. Meditation is God talking to us.

Part I

Colored orbs dance around my room at night. They are the spirits of my family and friends who have passed on to the next life. They are happy souls who bring guidance, support, strength, and love as they encourage me in my daily walk. They assure me of my purpose in this life—a purpose given by God; a purpose that took shape long ago and has grown throughout the years. It has been revealed as a gift of healing and spiritual growth.

1. The Early Years

I am eighty-three years old. Who would have ever guessed way back when—whenever "when" was—that life's journey would take me to a spiritual calling?

Everyone has a story to tell, and this is mine . . .

I was born the middle child of four children in the small mining town of Lead, South Dakota, in 1933. My older brothers were twins, Bob and Edward. Edward died at six months old of unknown causes. I also have a younger sister, Hazel. We lived in a small, one-story frame house near a creek. The water always ran black due to the residue runoff of the nearby gold mine. Tall pine trees stood near the house offering shade in the summer and some shelter from the cold wind in the winter. My grandmother, who I referred to as Mother, lived next door. She was my rock and I always felt closer to her than to my birth mother. Every morning, Bob and I would get dressed and run to her bedroom window. We would knock on the window and then run to the front door. She greeted us with a big smile and hug then led us to the kitchen, where she cooked the most wonderful breakfasts. She was a constant source of love, care, and support throughout my life. Her spirituality and faith were strong, and that strength, as well as her love and support, continues to this day from the spirit world.

Family Home (1935)
Lead, South Dakota

It was a stone's throw to Deadwood, one of the better-known and, at times, roughest towns of the Old West. Wild Bill Hickok, Lewis and Clark, Charlie Otter, Wyatt Earp, Calamity Jane, and many others frequented the area in their time. The town was still home to the Native Americans, particularly the Lakota/Sioux. These tribes lived there for hundreds of years among the mountains covered in dark ponderosa pines. The Lakota called it "Paha Sapa," meaning "Hills of Black." These "Black Hills" were estimated to have been fourteen thousand feet but have eroded to less than seven thousand feet, leaving outcroppings of gold ore, or leads (thus, the name of the town) in the granite that held North America's largest and deepest working gold mine, the Homestake Gold Mine. The mine provided employment and a livelihood for a good portion of the population, including my father. The Gold Rush ran from 1834 to 1876 with claims that gold was found on every creek in the northern Black Hills. When it closed in 2002, the mine had produced over 40 million ounces of gold—over one billion dollars in value—in its 125 years in operation.[1]

Much of this area was, and still is, sacred to the Sioux and other Native Americans. In 1868, the US government formulated a treaty, the Fort Laramie Treaty, establishing the Great Sioux Reservation, including all lands from the Mississippi River west to the Bighorn Mountains of western Wyoming. But, when gold was discovered in the Black Hills in 1874 by an expedition led by General George Custer, an invasion of miners hoping to strike it rich caused a gold rush that the US government could not control. The indigenous people were driven from their native land, their home. This inflamed an already deteriorating relationship between the Lakota/Sioux tribes and the white miners and settlers of the area.[2] The Sioux Nation demanded the government uphold the treaty, as it was their sacred land and they had legal rights to it.

Instead, the government offered the Sioux money in exchange for the land, but the Sioux refused. A court battle still ensues today for the ownership of the land.

Native American ceremonies are still performed there, even though the government prevents the exclusive use of the land for such. Bear Butte has been and continues to be the place for thousands of Native Americans to gather and pray. Sweat lodges, used for purification and treatment of disease, are available in an area set aside near the base of the mountain. All ceremonies of the Lakota/Sioux are for the good of the people, good living, improvement of self, and good health. It also teaches each to give back to Mother Earth and to be in balance with nature because the universe is vast and all should be in oneness with it.

---

[1] "Golden History," *Lead Area Chamber of Commerce*.
[2] Ibid.

Some of my earliest memories involve seeing Native Americans during the Days of '76, a celebration of the Gold Rush, in Deadwood. There were parades, bull riding, and rodeos. It lasted several days and is still an annual celebration attracting people from throughout the United States and Canada. Cowboys and Indians participated in the events, but my full attention was always on the Indians. When I was about four years old, I saw an Indian chief, dressed in full regalia with the long headdress and riding a beautiful, dappled-gray pony. I remember it as if it was yesterday. I was somewhat afraid of this powerful-looking man, but I was also filled with respect and admiration. I was somehow aware of the honor and integrity of this man's position and I could not shake his image from my mind.

Another memorable individual from the area was Potato Creek Johnny. Though he stood no more than four feet tall, his reputation was that of a giant. John Perrett migrated to the United States from Wales in 1883. Legend has it that Johnny discovered the world's largest gold nugget in Potato Creek, near Deadwood. Many said the nugget was actually several nuggets melted together, but it was never proven. Either way, he was quite a character. His short stature was accented by his long hair and beard. He certainly had the appearance of a die-hard prospector who loved to entertain visitors with his stories and tales of the gold hidden in the hills of Deadwood, South Dakota.

My childhood days were difficult for various reasons. However, I found time to play and enjoy being a child. Often, my brother Bob and I would pretend to be cowboys on stick horses. Those stick horses could run fast; or at least, we imagined it that way. We reenacted the scenes from movies at the local theatre. In the Black Hills of South Dakota, the theatre was not an elaborate establishment, but we enjoyed going from time to time. One afternoon, Bob and I got on our stick horses and rode into the hills accompanied by Rex, my grandmother's German shepherd dog. Time passed and we realized we were lost and didn't know how to get home. Rex did not seem concerned in the least and offered no help in our near-panic situation. I began to imagine that we were surrounded by Indians. They were hiding among the rocky cliffs, waiting to ambush us. I started to panic until I remembered the Indian chief I saw at the Days of '76 celebration. He seemed so honorable. I calmed myself by reasoning that the Indians were no different than me and posed no threat. Then, I decided to think like an Indian and convinced Bob to do the same. What would Indians do if they were lost? Soon, we found our tracks and followed them home.

Me and Bob and Rex (1937)
Black Hills

Many of my early experiences were learning events and crucial to my spiritual growth and self-awareness. One of the first of these was when I was five years old. I was playing with a hammer, trying to fix, or imagined that I was fixing, a broken wagon that slumped along the fence in front of the house. I carried that hammer around for hours as I worked and played outside.

After dinner, I went out to continue my work on the wagon. Opening the front door of the house, I noticed the hammer was not on the step where I had left it. I looked around the steps, thinking it may have fallen off onto the ground. It wasn't there. I checked under the porch where the dog usually slept. Maybe he had picked it up and carried it back to chew on it. It wasn't there either. After searching for two hours with no luck, it began to get dark outside and I had to go to bed. I was so distraught about losing my hammer that I had difficulty falling asleep. Hours passed before exhaustion overcame me and I drifted off. That night I had a vivid dream. It was so clear that I remember the details of the dream to this day. I saw myself walking along the fence from the house and up to the barn. The heat of the sun made my skin sizzle and my eyes squinted in the bright light. I smelled fresh-cut grass and heard the sound of horses pulling the plows in the nearby field. Following the wall of the barn, I brushed the rough wood with my fingers and stepped over high mounds of weeds that grew next to the barn. A pile of old, rusted tools lay at the end of the wall. There, on top of the pile, was my hammer, shining like a beacon. It shone as if it was on fire.

Lee (Left), Age 4
Bob, Age 6

The next morning, I quickly got dressed and ran outside. Following the directions of my dream, I approached the corner of the barn. I couldn't believe it. There it was. My hammer was lying on top of the pile of tools. How did it get there? I was not around this area of the barn the day before. My father had not left the house after dinner, so he couldn't have placed the hammer there. It remained a mystery to me until I was spiritually mature enough to realize that dreams are a way for Spirit to convey messages.

Other memories include Mother performing séances for people in the community. I remember one instance when a woman from the community was mourning her husband's sudden, unexpected death. She was tormented by the fear that he had crossed before making peace with God. Two months after his passing, she was so fatigued and depressed that she collapsed. Her children brought her to Mother to perform a séance in hopes that she would be able to contact the husband and assure their mother that he was indeed in Heaven. Mother welcomed them immediately and began the ceremony with prayers for guidance and God's love. The spirit of the woman's beloved husband soon joined them and assured his wife that not only was he in Heaven, but he was gloriously happy. Tears of joy streamed down the woman's face. Her husband was with God and she could be at peace. The family hugged Mother and expressed their appreciation for her help. Their heavy hearts had been filled with joy. I watched Mother as the family was leaving. She stood with her hands clasped together over her heart. A gentle smile formed on her lips and tears filled her eyes. She looked like an angel to me.

These are some of the memories that inspired me throughout my life. Mother had a special gift. I watched her share it with people in our community her entire life. I knew my birth mother also had a spiritual gift. It wouldn't be until later in my life that I would realize the tremendous spiritual gift I had been given.

My father, Byron Charles Hillberg, worked as a miner in the Homestake Gold Mine. He was called BC or Shorty. I refer to him as Shorty for reasons I will explain later. My mother, Mildred Leona, went to school to become a beautician. Later, she furthered her education and became a nurse. She was very bright and quick to learn new skills. Her small stature, five foot three, did not define her as she was strong willed and determined. I always said my mom was "full of fire." Her personality was quite different from her mother's, my grandmother. Like her mother, she had a spiritual gift, but did not exercise it in the same manner as Mother.

Picture of Spirits at Mother's Séance (1930)

Mother, my grandmother, was a major influence on my life. She was not an educated person but was one of the most intelligent people I have ever known. She was extremely gifted in the spiritual sense. God was prominent in her life and she gave credit and reverence to Him in all that she did. Day in and day out, she was the personification of devotion and dependability. Perhaps being raised in the Midwest in the early 1900s helped form these traits in her. She was born and raised in Parsons, Kansas, in 1898. Her father, Lafe Turner, worked fifty years for the Katy Railroad. Molly Turner, her mother, tirelessly worked the farm and cared for the family. The hard work and dedication of her family was embedded in her from the start.

My first encounters with spiritualism were watching Mother conduct séances and spiritual readings for people in order to communicate with their loved ones that had passed from this world. It was her way of using her gifts to comfort others and bring peace to their lives. It sparked a sense of spirit in me that supported me on my own journey. I was born with gifts of the spirit, just as everyone is, but my path was paved with my own unique, God-given abilities. I was given the gift of healing. Other family members who were a part of my daily life in the 1930s were Uncle Jim, who was in his late teens, and my grandfather Ed Harris. My grandfather was a kind and loving man. I was four years old when he passed away. I still remember the funeral services and how it was a major impact on the family.

These were difficult times. The Great Depression was raging due to the stock-market crash in 1929. Desperation filled the country as unemployment and hunger was the common condition for most people. Adding to the misery was an extended drought across most of the country. Throughout the 1930s, little rain and poor farming methods led to major erosion of the prairies. Strong winds picked up the dry soil and blew it across the land, creating "black blizzards" or "black rollers" that blackened the sky, turning daylight to dark.[3] The thick, blowing dust penetrated everything, including our lungs. Many developed health problems, especially respiratory diseases, and died.

---

[3] "Dust Bowl," *Wikipedia*.

Tumbleweeds would become wedged between the railings of fence, causing dirt to build up and form mounds. At times, the mounds would get so high the cattle would walk over the fences.

The Midwest became known as the Dust Bowl. Farming was almost impossible. Many gave it up for other means of supporting their families. Our saving grace was the Homestake Gold Mine. Employment remained fairly steady there and sheltered us from the brunt of the Depression. But, my father was growing tired of working in the gold mine due to the hard physical labor and dangerous conditions.

In 1938, my sister Hazel was born. Happily, Mom had completed her training as a beautician. My father had always wanted to be a farmer. Because of the effects of the Depression, land was cheap. So, my parents decided to buy a farm in Mitchell, South Dakota. But, to my dismay, it meant moving away from Mother.

Leaving Mother and the Black Hills was very difficult for me and my family. It became more difficult as time passed. Uncle Jim developed leukemia and died at the age of twenty. My grandfather, Ed, had only been gone for a short while, and Mother found the loss of her son, Jim, or Jimmy as she called him, a heavy weight to carry. But she remained in Lead and attempted to continue her life and spiritual work. Looking back, I am struck with her unfaltering faith and ability to persevere in the face of adversity.

2. Storm Clouds: Depression, Drought, and Hope

My family and I barely lived through this horrendous time beset by the Depression, results of the Dust Bowl, drought, swarming locusts, and family unrest.

It was 1939 and farming still involved plows and other equipment being pulled by horses. I had to learn to care for the horses as well as our cattle, pigs, and chickens. This daily routine was, of course, new to me, and it took some time to get used to. I missed my old life and I missed Mother. I really missed her morning hugs, smile, and the time spent with her over breakfast.

Lisbon #8
Lee, Age 8 (Far Right, Second Row)
Bob, Age 10 (Far Left, Second Row)

The school, Lisbon Number 8, was a mile-and-a-half walk for me and Bob. It was a one-room building that housed grades one through eight. We had one teacher for all grades, which totaled twelve to eighteen students. There was a barn for horses, if you were lucky enough to have one to ride to school. Not many did and it certainly was not a luxury we enjoyed. Our horses were needed at home to run the operation of the farm. In the winter, temperatures would drop to minus thirty degrees Fahrenheit. The classroom was heated by a wood-burning stove that the teacher would start every morning upon her arrival. On more than one occasion, my lunch froze. Drinking water was hand pumped from a well and carried in a bucket with a dipper for the children to drink from. There was no electricity or indoor plumbing so oil lamps and outhouses were a way of life at home and at school.

Bob, Lee
Ready for School (1939)

Discipline was not a problem. Parents, for the most part, took education very seriously. If you got in trouble at school, the teacher had the parents' permission to use corporal punishment. Most kids did not want to endure the pain and embarrassment of a public spanking. At least, not more than once. Unfortunately, the timing of our move from mining to farming was bad. The move brought many unforeseen changes to our lives. The biggest being that of going from a steady income to no income. Financial issues weighed heavily on us as we struggled day to day to make ends meet. The reign of the Dust Bowl still lingered, and would until the early 1940s. Iowa, Nebraska, South Dakota, and other parts of the Midwest suffered devastation, not only by the drought, but by an explosion in the population of grasshoppers. Grasshoppers undergo a transformation when conditions are dry. They normally live alone but, during droughts, they tend to congregate and form dense groups, or swarms. Sometimes, the swarms were so thick that they block the sunlight. This causes them to bump into each other, which, in turn, causes a hormonal shift in their bodies. They become locusts, social insects with ravenous appetites. Cornstalks, crops, tree leaves, any vegetation is eaten to the ground. Fields were left completely bare. Once the vegetation is devoured in one area, the swarm flies to its next meal, even if that meal is one hundred miles away.[4]

It was a time of economic and environmental crisis. There were no crops, there was no food, and there was no money. The government provided basic foods such as potatoes, beans, canned Spam, and dry foods to those in severe need. My family would drive to Mitchell monthly to pick up our portion of the relief. It was aid we appreciated but found difficult to accept. The Homestake Gold Mine had provided us with stability. We did not thrive, but we endured the Great Depression. We had food on our table. Now, as farmers, we barely survived on the government relief food and it hurt.

My father, Shorty's, behavior began to change. I am not sure if it was because of the hardships we endured after the move or if he was always that way and I couldn't see it because I was too

---

[4] Ibid.

young. But, he became angry. He had little education or social skills. His lack of compassion and short temper caused outbursts that ended with me or Bob being knocked to the floor. Most of the time, there was no apparent reason for his anger. Perhaps we didn't complete a task fast enough or fetch a tool fast enough. He would slap us on the back of the head or hit us with a razor strap. Shorty was the first bully I ever encountered. Although I was occasionally on the receiving end of his hot temper, Bob was his favorite target. Even Mom joined in on the angry outbursts toward us from time to time. The central theme of our family was fear.

Our early experiences tend to shape who we become. I became resistant to the abuse. Even though I was small and thin, my strong will kicked in and I was determined to fight for myself. I had self-respect and demanded respect from others. This served me well as I grew. I drove myself to be the best at everything whether it was sports, school, or hunting. This inner strength would help land me two state boxing championships. Ironically, Shorty would be the one who introduced me to the sport. Bob was different. The fearful family environment had a totally opposite effect on him. He developed low self-esteem, probably due to Shorty's abuse, which was both mental and physical. Instead of fighting back, he lost confidence in himself. His outlook on life had become clouded by Shorty. This was evident later. He lacked the motivation for success in school, as well as in career choices. He struggled to heal these wounds throughout his life.

We seldom practiced formal religion. Mother and Mom provided most of our guidance, with Mother taking the prominent role in spiritual matters. On occasion, our family attempted to gain guidance through the ouija, a board with the alphabet and other symbols used for contacting spirits. Bob and I followed our own path for help. We called on Edward, Bob's twin brother who died as a baby. We firmly believed in God and knew we could call on Him for help. But, Edward felt close and God seemed so far away.

Our farm was in disrepair, including the house. It was a two-story, wooden-frame structure in need of attention. The incessant wind would howl and whistle through the cracks around the windows. In the summer, it was a welcome breeze, but in the winter, it blew in snow, adding to the deep, piercing chill. A wood-burning stove required constant feeding in order to keep our family warm and cook our meals. Kerosene lamps provided light.

One night, when I was seven years old, I woke in the middle of the night to the vision of a man's face. The man appeared to be in his fifties, with dark hair and weathered skin. His stern expression was fixed and conveyed a look of determination. I remember thinking he must have been a hardworking man who spent years working the fields. The vision was crystal clear, as clear as if I was seeing it in daytime. I knew from watching Mother conduct séances that this was someone who had passed on into the afterlife. Even though I had been exposed to the spiritual world through Mother, I was still terrified. This was my first personal encounter with spirits and it changed me. That vision is still clear to me today.

December 7, 1941, is a day I will never forget. Our family gathered around the radio in the kitchen, listening to the report of the Japanese bombing of Pearl Harbor. I was so scared. As we listened to President Roosevelt deliver his speech, I wondered what would happen next. Japan attacked us on our own soil. What would this lead to?

Things started happening fast. War was raging and young American men started joining the military. We listened intently to the daily radio reports of the events in Europe and Japan. I did not quite understand it all but knew the war affected everyone. It became very clear to me, and everyone else, when we began rationing products that could be used by the military. The war changed our daily lives.

Everyone was very patriotic and did their part in helping our country in any way possible. We gathered scrap iron and other metals that were later melted and molded into military equipment. Willow branches were cut for making parachutes. Rationing of key products such as gas and tires and anything else that could be used to defend our nation was done without question.

In 1942, my family suffered another reeling blow. Our farm was repossessed. With the drought and meager production of crops, this was no surprise. We had no choice but to move again. This time, we rented land north of Mitchell. We shared crops with the landowner and took out a loan with the Federal Land Bank to purchase farm equipment. We bought a well-used John Deere tractor, plows, and some planters.

Due to the war effort, many men joined the military. This resulted in farmers having more land to cultivate. More land and better equipment meant greater productivity. Combine this with rain, and you had a winning combination. We were finally blessed with a plentiful harvest of corn, wheat, and oats. Grass grew well, producing hay to feed cattle. Most farmers also raised large numbers of chickens, turkeys, and hogs. Money was still limited but farming was profitable again and we were thankful.

Bob and I worked on the farm when we were not in school. I took care of the livestock, milked the cows, and cared for the ducks and chickens. I had severe hay fever so my work in the field was limited. Bob worked in the fields and drove the tractor for planting and harvesting the crops. We also had a large garden that supplied us with enough vegetables to last all year. My mother would can fresh vegetables and meat. She also dried corn for use during the winter. We had enough to eat and times were good.

As far as I was concerned, farming wasn't the only thing that had improved. School was a much better experience for me. It was consolidated with grades one through twelve but we didn't have to walk to school anymore. We were bussed to and from school. This was such a welcome change, especially in the harsh winters.

By the time I was nine years old, my hunting skills were so good that I was given the responsibility of bringing home the wild game for the dinner table. I was an adept trapper and a keen marksman with the rifle. I became a crack shot out of necessity because ammunition was expensive. The rule was "one shot, one bird equals dinner." In the winter, I would set trap lines for animals such as rabbits, skunks, badgers, and muskrats. Some were sold for their fur and some for their meat. Migratory birds like ducks and geese were plentiful in the fall. South Dakota was well known for its pheasant population and their meat made an enjoyable dinner.

Fishing was another method of putting food on the table. In the summer, the lakes were also good for swimming. Bob and I didn't get much free time away from the farm, but when we did, we would head for the lake.

I enjoyed the outdoors even though the weather in South Dakota could be very harsh. Hot summers and cold winters still found me outside as much as possible. I liked to watch animals and take in the beauty of nature. Flocks of ducks or geese flying high overhead or cattle grazing in the field were sources of wonder and enjoyment for me. They were part of Creation and I always felt a connection to them. I was at my best when I was outside. Even then, I was joined with the Indian spirit but did not realize it. My grandfather, Jim, often stated that "Lee rides like an Indian and can shoot from horseback."

The wind was always blowing. I often said that I didn't know the wind was blowing until it stopped one day. To an extent, it was an annoyance. Rain, dirt, and snow in a driving wind could make conditions quite unbearable. But, on the other hand, the wind also generated power to pump water from the wells. When there was no wind, the water was drawn by hand. Needless to say, pumping water by hand was tiring when supplying water for people and livestock.

By the time I was in the eighth grade, the war was over and our country enjoyed peace. Farmers were doing well and the poverty we suffered earlier had subsided. Life was somewhat easier and the future looked brighter. It seemed that God was smiling on us all.

One day, Shorty told me and Bob about a boxing team that had formed in town and he wanted us to be a part of it. Bob wanted nothing to do with it. Boxing was not in his DNA. He avoided conflict at all costs. I, however, agreed to join the team. It was Shorty's idea, not mine, but I thought it wouldn't hurt to learn some additional skills. It could come in handy since I was no stranger to fights at school. Apparently, using my fist to make friends and influence people was in my DNA. But, being a small kid and slightly frail, no one took me as a threat. Maybe Shorty figured I would benefit from the training and discipline of the ring. He had no experience in boxing. Why was he adamant that Bob and I learn the sport? Perhaps he was living vicariously through us in order to satisfy some lost dream of his own youth. Maybe it was the bully in him that enjoyed the physical exchange. I didn't know the answer but decided that it didn't matter.

The team was called the United Commercial Travelers. We trained in the Corn Palace facility in Mitchell and Shorty made sure I got to practice. We had two coaches. They set up matches with other teams throughout the state. Many of our members were soldiers who returned from war with boxing experience. Some of these young men were in their twenties and there I was, at thirteen years old, holding my own in the ring with them.

Patch from Boxing Jacket

My dedication and hard work paid off. I won two State Golden Glove Championships. I no longer had to fight for the respect of others. I was amazed at how many people in town would point at me and say, "Hey, there's the Champ." I enjoyed the recognition. It was a big deal and I was proud of what I had accomplished.

It was clear to me that I did not want to be a farmer for the rest of my life. I realized that if I was going to pursue another career, other than farming, I was going to have to be the best in other aspects of my life, not just boxing. So, I constantly pushed myself at school. I enjoyed hunting, baseball, and track and I was good at them. In my senior year, I was elected captain of the track team. But academics were my top priorities. I knew I wanted another way of life. I knew I was capable of being anything I wanted to be and I would accept nothing less for myself. I worked hard for high grades and looked forward to college.

Golden Gloves State Champions (1947)
Lee (Far Right)

Several of my high school teachers were great influences on me. They taught me to strive for excellence but also balance hard work with fun. They recognized my dreams and nudged me toward leadership positions. They suggested that I run for student government. I decided to run for president. If I was going to jump into something, I might as well jump in with both feet. I won the election and spent the next year managing relations between the school faculty and student body. It was enjoyable and a great learning experience for me. Later, I was also elected to attend Boys State, sponsored by the American Legion. It was, and still is, a highly regarded government education program for high school students. One had to be nominated by their teachers and then win the final election to attend.

These were positive points in my life that contributed to my confidence and helped mold me into the successful man I would become. Politics were not in my future, but some high-level management was in my journey ahead.

My Sister Hazel

3. The Military

Sometimes an opportunity comes along that has your name on it. That was the air force for me. I always knew I would leave rural South Dakota, and this was my ticket. The training I received and the furthering of my education opened up the world for me.

After graduating from high school, I worked for the US Forest Service, in Idaho, during the summer and went to college during the school year. I finished my second summer with the Forest Service and was getting ready to return to college when I was reclassified for the draft. The Korean War was in full swing. American forces allied with South Korea in order to resist the spread of communism. Basically, this was the start of the Cold War with Russia and China. The Selective Service, or draft, used a lottery system based on birthdates to select young American males for military service. If selected, you were required by law to serve in the military. Those who tried to "dodge" or avoid the draft were sent to prison. However, it allowed you to defer or change your classification to a lower status if you were attending college. It lessened your chances of being "called up" and shipped out, at least for the immediate future. I chose not to defer. Money was short and I enlisted in the air force. This would make me eligible for the GI Bill later, which would pay for my college education.

I completed basic training in Lackland, Texas. From there, I went to Keesler Air Force Base in Mississippi for electronics training. This led me into electronics and radar technology. My ground-radar-surveillance training was at the AC&W Radar Site and airborne radar training was at AWAC McClellan Air Force Base, both in California. I became an AEW radar-maintenance technician.

Basic Training
Lackland Air Force Base
Lee on Right (1952)

Promotions were based on merit and time accrued in the air force. I earned the rank of staff sergeant in a short period of time due to my ability to decipher and maneuver through the logistical, more intricate schematics of the radar systems.

As a radar technician with the 552nd AEWCW, I serviced the radar and other electronic equipment on the RC 121-D Constellation aircraft, or "Connie," as we called it. It was a flying radar station used, among other things, to identify "friend or foe." Whether Connie was on the ground or in flight, my job was to keep the radar, which was radioactive, and electronic equipment running. I also supervised fifty to a hundred airmen. While on the ground, I was known as the NCO, or noncommissioned officer, and while in flight, I was the first tech.

The Cold War was in full swing and our missions were to provide air defense to the West Coast of the United States. We flew for twelve hours in orbits, or oval patterns several miles off the West Coast, looking for enemy aircraft. Our squadron was on high alert twenty-four hours a day, three hundred sixty-five days a year. If we picked up an unidentified aircraft on radar, a jet fighter was scrambled immediately to intercept it before it could pose a threat to US airspace. There were missions where the twelve hours stretched to twenty-four or even twenty-six hours from preflight to postflight. Thankfully, the Connie was equipped with bunk beds so we could grab a quick nap if necessary.

Keeping the electronics working on the aircraft was critical to our missions. If there was an equipment failure, we only had a certain amount of time to repair it before the mission was aborted and another aircraft deployed in its place. Aborting a mission was grievous because it left the country at high risk due to the loss of radar coverage. It was also expensive due to dumping fuel and sending up another airplane and crew to replace it.

One of the RC 121-D airplanes, or Connies, my squadron flew came in new from Lockheed with the tail identification of 555. We called it the Triple Nickel. From the beginning, it had mechanical and electronic problems. Something was always failing on that airplane. It quickly became known as the "spook plane." I spent the duration of most missions repairing one thing and then another. It was always a question of "what next." About two months before my discharge from the air force, I flew a mission on Triple Nickel with several engineers from Lockheed and various other aircraft manufacturers. They were there to evaluate the faults occurring with this plane. We actually completed the mission without any major issues or failures. But as we left our orbit and started for the base, the alternator failed. This, obviously, was not my area of expertise and could not be fixed in flight since it was in the engine. We made it home and landed safely. But I am sure those engineers had quite a conversation about their flight with us.

In my 3,500 hours of flight-time service, including my service on Triple Nickel, only two missions were aborted due to electronic failure. This record is something that I am very proud of as it was rare among first techs. And I will say that Triple Nickel must have worked out the kinks in the system because it went on to be the first to control the shooting down of an enemy MIG aircraft. Today, it is housed in the Air Force Museum on Wright-Patterson Air Force Base in Dayton, Ohio.

Staff Sergeant USAF

Crew Member Wings
Over 3,500 Hours Flight Time

I fully enjoyed my time in the air force. They were my family and the experience was nothing short of outstanding. It provided invaluable education, training in a high-level technical electronics field, leadership experience, and promotions on merit that would give me a head start in my career. The air force was a very good growth and educational experience for me.

4. The Business Years

Lee will grow into a strong life and live in a very nice house. He will work in something connected to radio.
—Mother, 1930

Thus far, my achievements are greater than I ever dreamed possible. I had always worked hard. Now, my hard work was paying off.

Coming from the air force, RCA Corporation was a good fit for me. I spent sixteen years in middle-level management with them. Being an executive meant that I would have to move often and travel a lot. I was married with two children. It was difficult on all of us, but necessary at the time. We lived in Texas, New Jersey, and Pennsylvania. I was also required to continue my education. I took courses at Duke University and University of Chicago as well as special management courses taught by RCA.

RCA contracted with the air force, navy, and State Department to design and develop electronic technology to assist in the war effort. Several projects challenged my technical and management skills, particularly those that sent me to parts of the world where English wasn't spoken. Over the years, I went to Vietnam, South America, Africa, Japan, and Mexico.

Da Nang Air Force Base
Vietnam (1963)

Radar Tower on Monkey Mountain
Vietnam (1963)

One of the most challenging and stressful projects was in Vietnam during the Vietnam War. RCA was contracted to design and install a ground radar site on Monkey Mountain in Da Nang, Vietnam. The radar would monitor the airspace between North and South Vietnam. This would give the United States control and guidance for its own aircraft and the ability to identify enemy aircraft over the region. My assignment was to survey the site, complete the design layout, and obtain approval for the plan from the US Air Force. I flew to Vietnam, on US government orders, aboard an air-force military air-transport services, or MATS, aircraft. Two days after my arrival in Saigon, news of an American civilian contract representative being captured in North Vietnam was all over the news. Since I was there in that capacity, many people at home were worried that I was the one that had been captured. This made me reassess the reality of who I was and where I was, politically speaking.

It was obvious that the whole region was on high alert. Guards with machine guns stood watch everywhere. No one trusted anyone. I knew that it was in my own best interest to remain on high alert as well.

One of my first tasks in Saigon was to meet with US and South Vietnamese Air Force officers to discuss the job on Monkey

Mountain. Since I didn't speak Vietnamese or French, their other language, and needed to take a taxi, I had the US personnel at Bachelor Officers Quarters, where I was staying, write down my origination and destination addresses. I had taken the trip once before and thought it would eliminate the language barrier with the taxi driver. The taxi was hailed and I gave the driver the paper with the address. He nodded and we were on our way. Before I knew it, we were in a strange area and moving at a high rate of speed. I didn't recognize anything from my previous trip to the meeting site. Something told me that this was bad, really bad. I knew the word "stop" in Vietnamese and shouted it at the driver. He ignored me and kept going. Fear and rage took over as I reached forward and grabbed the reckless bloke by the shirt collar and demanded he comply with my order. I am not sure if it was the death grip I had on his collar or the menacing look in my eyes, but he stopped the car. His eyes were the size of saucers and sweat began to bead on his upper lip. I could see that he understood me well. I still had him by the collar. I pointed at the BOQ origination address and he nodded again. I released my hold on him and he eased the car back on the road. Minutes later, I was back at the BOQ hailing another taxi. This time, I arrived at the meeting without incident.

This assignment was difficult in many ways but I finally completed the work and began making plans to fly home with the US Air Force. In order to leave the country, I needed an exit visa from South Vietnam. I went to the Vietnamese agency to obtain it and was inundated with a mountain of paperwork. I would submit one document and he would give me three more. The pile of papers grew larger and larger until I said enough and left. I thought the US Embassy should be able to help me in getting out of this nightmare. I explained what happened to the embassy agent and was told that the Vietnamese clerk was looking for a bribe. It was common for the local officials there to make the visa process an agonizing experience unless you greased their palms with a little monetary incentive. I had no intention of playing their game and relied on the US Embassy to get me out. They got the necessary papers filed and soon I was on my way home. As harrowing as it was, my job was done and the air force had approved the radar-site plans.

Lee
Saigon (1963)

RCA also contracted with the government of Paraguay to install five international communication links via transmitter-and-receiver sites in the jungle outside the town of Asuncion. Cable was buried in the ground and ran for several miles between these locations.

Electrical power was supplied by remote diesel generators. Since the site would not operate without electricity, there were three generators. The main generator was online, the second was on "hot" standby, and the third was "cold" standby. For unknown reasons, the generators were failing. Our division vice president needed an experienced engineer to fly to the site, evaluate the problem, and fix it. After much discussion, meetings, and investigation no one had solved the issue.

One day, I attended one of the meetings with the vice president on the Paraguay project. Being aware of the ongoing technical problems, I had studied the schematics and had an idea that it might be a timing issue. I was not a design engineer and had no experience in basic circuit design. But I had a knack for the intricate workings of electrical systems and timing circuits, which had served me well in the air force. During the meeting, I kept feeling that I was being prodded to volunteer to assist in the site repairs. I finally spoke up and said, "I can fix it." A few days later, I was on my way to Paraguay.

I worked twenty-hour days analyzing and testing the system at the site. I designed new circuits and ordered new parts. When they arrived, I installed them. The repairs were completed and the generators were turned on again. To no surprise, they worked. All I had to do then was put together a training program on a system I had never been trained on, teach the staff how to operate and maintain the equipment that no one ever taught me to use, and return to my "real" job at home.

There was no mystery as to how I was able to do this without previous training. I had never seen or used this type of equipment before this trip. Yet I was confident in my assessment and analysis. The entire time, I felt I was being guided by Spirit. I knew, without a doubt, that I would be successful in this endeavor. It was a great accomplishment and it gave me a new insight and appreciation of my spiritual background. Spirit used me to bring about good in the world and I was thankful.

Later in my career with RCA, I was assigned a State Department project in the Republic of Guinea, Africa. This time, I had an assistant with me. He was a photographer and fluent in French. We were to survey and photograph various airports for the design and installation of a ground-to-air, or airport-to-aircraft, communication system.

When we arrived and were deboarding the airplane in Guinea, I was pulled from the passengers by the Guinean police and taken to a separate room for questioning. What was my purpose for being there? What was I going to do while in Guinea? I was concerned that I was the focus of attention even though there were many people on the flight. Maybe it was just the luck of the draw and they chose me at random. It was probably a routine procedure that shouldn't cause me alarm. But whatever their reason was, I was alarmed. This trip was off to a bad start. I was being detained by police in a foreign communist country that was known for political instability and unrest. Still, I remained calm and answered their questions with the help of my assistant. After their interrogation, they searched my luggage. Finding nothing of interest to them, I was released and we went to our hotel.

A few days later, there was a letter in my hotel mailbox commanding me to report to the local police station. A cold chill ran up the back of my neck. It must not have been a random selection that pulled me out at the airport. Something about this project raised a red flag with them. I knew that it would be a mistake to abide by this ominous request. I reported this to the US Embassy instead. I was told to go about my business, but be cautious.

We had completed three airport surveys and were deep into the country when our passports and airline tickets were confiscated by the police. We were forced to stay in our hotel room and wait. There was no glass or screens over the small windows. It was hot and there was little air movement. Insects came in and out freely. The only water was from the faucets and it was contaminated. We had quinine pills from the US to purify the water so we could drink it without getting sick. Three miserable days passed before the Guinean authorities returned our passports and airline tickets to us.

We still had work to do. After being stuck in our hotel room for three days, we were pushed to complete the remaining airport surveys. It wasn't something that could be rushed as it required attention to detail and travel time. But this was one project that tested my patience and endurance. I couldn't wait to get home.

At one of the airport sites near the ocean, several of Guinea's engineers asked me many technical questions about radio transmissions. I was intrigued and suspicious at the same time. After some discussion, I learned that the Guinea government was building a high-powered radio station nearby. I asked them to take us to the site. They agreed and soon I knew why my suspicions had been raised. The power output on the radio station was much higher than they had described. I asked them if we could take a few photos. They allowed it since they wanted my input on their design, location, and the effect of the nearby mountains on their transmissions. I immediately reported my findings to the US Embassy. They were totally unaware of the station's existence. They later discovered that the station was built to broadcast propaganda to the neighboring countries as an attempt to spread communism.

After returning to the United States, the photos of the Guinean radio station were sent to be developed. Mysteriously, they disappeared and I never saw them or knew what happened to them. But, shortly thereafter, I received a visit from a CIA agent. He was very interested in my trip to Guinea and the radio station they were building. I told him about being detained at the airport, the letter from the police, the three days in the hotel room, and all of the details on the radio station. He listened intently but provided no other feedback on these findings.

Several months later, the division vice president of RCA called me to his office. I couldn't think of any reason why he would want to see me at that time. As far as I knew, all was well and there was nothing critical to report. I couldn't help but wonder what was so important that the vice president needed to see me. When I entered his office, I was greeted by another agent from the CIA. I was being recognized for my help in exposing the Guinean radio station as a communist ploy. He read a letter of commendation to me but could not give me a copy due to the sensitivity of the content.

Arriving in New Delhi, India, for Business Meetings

Bombay, India

Dinner Meeting with Indian Officials

Taj Mahal
Agra, India

Any subsequent trips I made outside of the United States after that was followed up by a visit from the CIA. Over the years, I had several visits from them and was always eager to help our country in any way possible. There was a project I was working on for the navy that required me to hold a much higher security clearance than what I had. The navy officer in charge said that the level I needed was difficult to obtain and would take a long time to be approved. Maybe it was difficult in most cases, but I was approved in a matter of days. It's nice to know people in high places.

Part II

5. Transition to Spirituality

> *My spiritual awakening has been sudden after being dormant for a number of years! I have embraced it with elation and accepted its life-changing momentum. I am being given more guidance from Spirit in the nature of visions, dreams, and intuition. Indians walk with me in the woods. What a wonderful world! All of my past life, everything I've experienced, has brought me to this point in time.*

When I was thirty-seven years old, I was living in New Jersey. I started practicing Christianity and became involved in church and other civic organizations. I was appointed a lay leadership position at the church I had been attending for several years. I assisted in worship services, pastoral care, and administrative operations.

It was time for my routine medical exams so I scheduled an appointment with my doctor. We chatted as he checked my vital signs and did the usual things a doctor does during a physical exam. A few days later, I got a call from his office saying that he had my results and asked that I come into the office to review them. I didn't give it much thought as I was busy and felt fine. Two days later, I was sitting in his office listening to words that I was not prepared to hear: "You have cancer."

My life changed dramatically at the moment I heard the word "cancer." The plans I had at work and at home were suddenly pushed aside in order to deal with something that would threaten my entire existence. It forced itself ahead of everything else. It was an unwanted priority that I had to face with the tenacity and faith I was yet to test. Fortunately, I lived near Philadelphia, Pennsylvania, so treatment was close. Following doctors' orders, I underwent surgery and then radiation treatment.

On the last day of radiation therapy, I was sitting in the waiting room when I became filled with a warm glow that felt like gold light.

"I became filled with a warm glow that felt like gold light."

I intuitively knew that gold was good. I didn't know then that the color gold stimulates the immune system and heightens enthusiasm. But it filled me with a sense of hope and well-being. My upbringing with Mother told me that this was Spirit telling me that I was going to be all right. It was a strong, powerful message that left me relieved, thankful, and at peace. A year later, the cancer was back . . . but I wasn't afraid. This was only a glitch, a temporary setback. Glitches do not affect Spirit. Spirit told me that I would be healed and I knew, without a doubt, that I would be cured. We proceeded with treatment plans. My body would not tolerate any more radiation, so I underwent chemotherapy. The treatment lasted several months and, during that time, my company offered me a position in Boston. Relocation and moving were difficult when I was in good health. They would certainly be even more so during my treatments. However, God and Spirit gave me the confidence to proceed with the move.

In a short time, I was living in Boston and cancer free. I thanked God for my healing because, as I stated before, all healing is from Him.

Life went on and I maintained my career, as well as stayed involved in my children's lives. I attended school functions and coached baseball, swimming, and lacrosse. Education was important and I supported my children and my wife in their academic careers. Both of my children earned college degrees and my wife earned her master's in education. I am happy that I was able to provide that foundation for them.

During all of those years, I had no contact with Shorty, my father. When he died, I did not return to South Dakota for the funeral services. Forgiveness was not easy for me. The feelings of fear and anger lingered and I carried them with me for too long. As my spiritual journey progressed, I was finally able to fully forgive him. This will be discussed later.

I was sixty-three years old and vice president of a major company in the United States. Stress from the high-level position, business reductions, cost cuts, technological changes, travel, and too many relocations took its toll. I was successful, respected, and financially secure. My boyhood dreams had all come true. It was time to leave the corporate world and start a new course, a new direction in life.

Not everything in retirement was as I planned. Shortly after retiring, I went through a divorce. I later tried marriage for the second time and went through divorce for the second time. It was extremely painful and I began to look at life in a different way. I withdrew from organized religion but retained my core belief in God and the afterlife. That has never changed and never will. My faith remains strong as well as my spiritual experiences, which all center around God. As a matter of fact, both have grown stronger and continue to deepen to this day. It is said that the most difficult experiences lead to the greatest learning and growth. I believe and I know this is true.

My retirement was never going to be an extended couch time. I needed and wanted to stay busy. I joined the local library and studied the Civil War, world religions, plants, trees, and Native Americans. I became an authority on Native American history and culture. I conducted talks and presentations on the subject. I filled my days being productive and positive.

I have always had a deep love for nature. Trees, plants, animals, and birds all hold significance to me. Any postretirement employment had to involve working outside. For instance, I was once a marshall for a golf course. As you can imagine, most days were uneventful. Sometimes you had to run a few gophers, the two-legged kind, off the greens. Or, occasionally, deal with theft and vandalism. Some days, I would get in a few holes of golf myself.

Another job was with a landscaping company selling plants, flowers, and trees. It was during this time I met a woman, Billie, who had lost her husband to cancer several years earlier. She had been seeking peace and opportunities to fill her life in a positive way. In her search, she had become an avid reader and read many books on spiritualism and metaphysics. She also acquired healing through the readings and spiritual guidance of a professional medium and intuitive psychic, Carolyn Cummings. Since my grandmother had been a spiritual medium, I immediately felt a connection with Billie. She was a wealth of information on the subject and I was eager to learn from her. Spiritualism was a natural link between us. She provided me with books to read and we would discuss them along with our own experiences. I had grown up with spiritualism but mostly as a spectator. Now,

I was ready to be an active participant. Billie and I were very compatible and our relationship remains strong to this day.

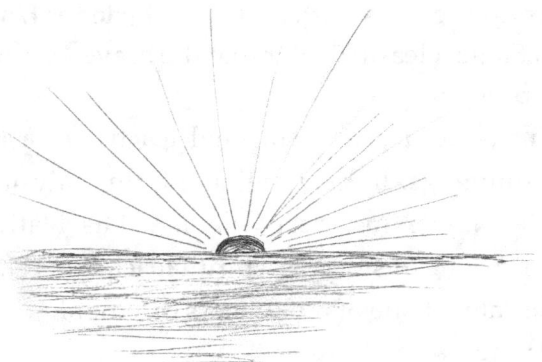

New Life, New Horizons

As I became more connected to Spirit, I began to receive some very special visions and guidance. During a very stressful time, I was spending quiet, thoughtful time in the living room. Standing next to the fireplace with my right hand on the mantle, I intuitively heard, "Stand tall." I knew it was Mother sending her encouragement to me as I struggled through this difficult situation.

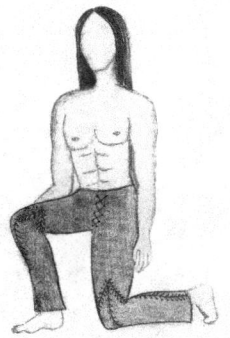

Indian Brave

A short time later, during meditation, I received a very clear and powerful vision. An Indian brave was kneeling on the ground. He was in his early twenties, lean, long black hair, and wore deerskin breeches with no shirt. The letter E appeared so I called him Eagle. I learned later that the brave was actually me in one of my previous lives.

I was introduced to my spiritual teacher in a reading with Carolyn Cummings. In his time here in the physical world, he had been a Native American shaman. His Native American family had a long history as spiritual leaders. His name was given to me later at one of my prayers ceremonies: Ax. He is with me all the time.

6. Native Americans

Having grown up in Native American territory, I knew something of their belief system and culture, which engendered a strong kinship and connection in me to them and their way of life.

When I got older, I became a student of the Muskogee/ Creek, as they once lived where I now live. As my knowledge grew, so did my bond with them. They were self-sufficient people making their way in an unfriendly world. They were honorable, revered and respected all of that which is nature, and were extremely spiritual.

When researching and studying the Muskogee/Creek Indians, it is important to look to their origins. These Native Americans were believed to be from Mongolian descent in Northwestern Asia. They migrated across the Bering Strait land bridge during the last Ice Age about twenty thousand years ago.

Archeological evidence shows small bands of wandering hunters reached the eastern woodlands of North America about 12,000 BC. These nomadic bands, which were small groups and families, spread across North America all the way to Northern Alabama and Northwest Georgia where they established villages, or settlements.

Life was difficult but animals provided food, skins for clothing, and bones for making tools. As they traveled farther southeast, large animals began to disappear and were replaced by smaller animals such as brown bears, the white-tailed deer, rabbits, and turkeys. This would prove more challenging for supplying food as they were accustomed to one large animal providing sustenance for their entire group. However, plants were becoming more plentiful as the climate became milder. The growing season came early and lasted late into the year. They learned to plant and harvest seeds, which was a major change in their way of life. These early agriculturists became quite skillful at cultivating plants for food and medicinal purposes. Corn, beans, and squash was a major part of their diet. They learned that the combination of beans and corn provided plant protein and could make up for the decline in animal meat. They would plant not only in fields, but throughout wooded areas. They would live in that area until the soil was depleted of nutrients, then move to a more fertile area.

They had no written method of communication until the late 1820s so all learning was passed down orally from generation to generation. Trade with other bands or tribes was very beneficial in exchanging of goods and sharing of traditions and cultures. Travel was by way of footpaths through the wilderness, waterways, and rivers.

Clans, Villages, Tribes, and Government

The basic unit of social organization among the Creeks was the clan, a tightly knit group of blood relatives whose descent was traced through the mothers. Almost all Creeks belonged to clans. Even war captives sought to be adopted by a clan. Clan membership extended across village lines and throughout the Creek Nation. All members were required to defend and support each other at all times. In sickness or health, they shared the responsibility of rearing children, caring for the elderly and homeless, and tending to daily chores. Each family had their own plot of land and planted their own crops. In addition, there was a larger village garden where all members shared in the cultivation work.

There seems to have been a strictly enforced sanction on intermarriage. No one could marry another member of the same clan. All clans were named after animals or elements of nature. Nine clans—Wind, Bear, Bird, Beaver, Raccoon, Alligator, Water Moccasin, Deer, and Panther—are still powerful among the Creek today.

They governed themselves in surprisingly complex and organized societies. Committees were established and run by a "miko" who, along with a council of elders, made most of the decisions. All villages were organized around a public square that was oriented to depict the four cardinal directions of east, west, north, and south. Structures, called tuplas, were made of mud and cane and had a thatched roof.

The practice of "an eye for an eye" was enforced without exception. Should an injury occur on a clan member, even accidentally, the males were required to exact punishment of equal proportion on the assailant. This policy included women, children, and the elderly and it was rarely waived.

Spiritual Beliefs

The Creeks were, and still are, a very spiritual people. They believed in a supreme being, a living god whose name in Creek was "Kun Kushula." In the English translation, it meant "Master of Breath." They venerated the sun, moon, and wind as well as all of nature. They saw humankind as part of nature and no more important than the other elements of creation. As nature was divine, fundamental in all things spiritual and physical, it was paramount to be in pure and constant balance with it.

They believed that people and animals had souls and, after death, traveled to the west on "Spirits Road." They also believed in mythical beings that played a vital part in their daily lives. However, they had no concept of heaven or hell.

The spiritual leaders and healers were selected by the elders and other established leaders of the tribe. Those selected were usually young males and, sometimes, women. These potential leaders, sometimes called shamans or medicine men, underwent extensive training including the study of plants and formulas used in making medicine for healing. Many plants used as cures by the Creeks are still used today and distributed through our pharmacies. They also learned songs and chants for the spiritual ceremonies. At the completion of their training, they participated in a ritual of rebirth. The newly appointed healer or medicine man/shaman could then wear an owl feather in his or her headdress, depicting their new power.

Special individuals called "knowers" were considered by the Creek to be vested with spiritual powers far beyond the normal. A "knower" was not a shaman, medicine man, or priest. He was considered to have the combined knowledge and power of all three.

Many objects were thought to possess special powers and treated with great respect. Rocks, especially crystals, were considered good medicine for hunting and war. Feathers were used in all ceremonies, attached to hunting equipment, and worn as part of attire, for example, a headdress. The eagle feather was considered sacred and used in spiritual ceremonies.

Sometime after 1000 BC, life for the Native Americans began to improve and they were able to think beyond the daily struggles for survival. A new culture emerged and they began to place special emphasis on burial of their dead. They held funeral ceremonies and burial mound traditions. Mounds were built for other purposes as well. The purpose of the ceremony dictated the height and width of the mound. Platform and temple mounds of the South were used in many cultures and at different times and for various ceremonial purposes. Some sites show a history of continuous usage for a period of over two thousand years. This culture was termed "Mississippian" and was influenced by Central America.

There are many Indian mound complexes in North America. The Adena Hopewell dates from 1000 BC to 1000 AD; Mississippi mounds date 700 AD to 1700 AD. In the state of Georgia, there are two which can be visited today. The Etowah Indian Mound State Historical Site in Cartersville and the Kolomoki Mound State Park in Early County. Both of these served the Mississippian and late Woodland cultures. It should be noted that Thomas Jefferson was one of the first to document Indian mound building and its history.

Social Customs

Descent among the Creek Indians was determined matrimonially and the men moved to the clan and tupa of his wife. Children were dominated by the mother and her blood relations. This also meant the children belonged to the mother's village, known as the "tulwa."

No matter what time of year or what the weather conditions were, the Creek children were born out of doors in huts, or "tupas." These tupas were a short distance from the family living quarters. The women entered the hut alone, gave birth alone, and remained alone with the child for a specified length of time after the birth.

Boys and girls were treated differently from birth. Throughout their lives, they were confined to rigid, separate roles based on tradition, sex, and the struggle to survive. The boys grew up to be hunters and warriors. They were proud and strong, showing no fear even to death. The girls, out of necessity spurred from enduring in the elements, remained equally fearless and tough.

Young and old alike enjoyed music and dancing. They were always part of their ceremonies. Some of the dances were animal dances, stomp dances, and peace dances. The stomp dance, a European name describing the rhythmic steps performed by the dancers, was one of the most important sacred and social dances of many Southeastern tribes. The Creek called it "Opvnku Haco," or "dance of the altered state." It is still practiced today in association with the "Poskeeta," known as the Green Corn Ceremony. This ceremony and its significance will be discussed later in Chapter 7. It is like Christmas, Thanksgiving, New Year's Day, and Mardi Gras all rolled into one ceremony in late summer. The dance is accompanied by singing, chanting, and musical instruments such as drums, rattles, clapper sticks, and flutes. A ceremonial speaker calls participants to each round of the dance. Afterward, "touch medicine" is practiced. The participants "touch" the medicine, bringing healing and spiritual well-being throughout the community.

The most popular pastime for men, when time was available, was "ball play" or "brother at war," which was a game that resembled modern lacrosse and almost every tulwa had a team. There were fifty to a hundred men on each side. The game is still played today among the Creeks. They also wrestled and held footraces. Gambling on the games were common and all played with full vigor and the eagerness to win. For women, more domestic crafts were practiced including weaving, carving, sewing, pottery, and tanning hides.

Time and space, as well as distance, were dependent upon natural elements such as sunrise, sunset, the moon, and sleep patterns. Distance was also measured by sight. Generally, as far as one could see would be the equivalent of our mile.

The Muskogee/Creek Indians developed a way of life that persevered from 1000 BC until the Europeans made contact in the seventeenth century, a period of about 2,500 years. It is important to realize that their lives were based on a subsistent economy, not a surplus economy. The people took from nature only that which was necessary to survive. Waste was not tolerated.

This was a belief system whose very essence meant balance and harmony with all of nature. They were in awe of nature and its abundance—the sun, moon, wind, water, fire, sky, plants, and animals. This was their life.

Early explorers such as Juan Ponce de Leon and Hernando de Soto came to the New World, the homeland of the Native Americans, with the intentions of gathering wealth and spreading Christianity. They brought many new, useful tools and weapons with them. They also introduced the horse to North America. However, the Native Americans paid a very high price for these conveniences.

At first, the Native Americans were hospitable to the Europeans. They shared their resources and exchanged ideas and trinkets. As time passed, however, it became evident that the settlers would not be content with a coexistence. They began to force their ideology and beliefs on the Native Americans, wanting to change the very foundation of the Indian culture. In the eyes of the Creeks, admitting one change in the system would cause a ripple effect in the entire system challenging everything. A major difference between Christianity and the Creek spiritual belief was in relationship to the natural world. The Native American belief system emphasized order, analogy, similarity, balance, purity, and peace. It was totally tolerant. Christianity tends to teach to overcome, control, and exploit. These opposing views caused a deep, fundamental discord between the Native Americans and European settlers. The settlers thought they had dominion over nature and the Creeks vehemently disagreed.

The profound consequence of the Creeks' closed, or adamant, belief system limited their ability to maintain their own stability and respond to the challenges of the settlers. Native Americans came to view the European settlers as profoundly immoral, ignorant, and without proper hygiene. They thought, in short, that the Europeans were savages. In turn, the Europeans viewed the Native Americans as uneducated savages. Carrying advanced weapons and diseases the Native Americans had no immunity to fight, the European settlers prevailed. They implemented a long and painful coup that would abolish the established freedom and peace the Native Americans based their lives upon. The Europeans enslaved the Indians, taking away the freedom that was so vital to them and their way of life. By far, the most devastation brought to the Indians were the diseases such as smallpox, influenza, diphtheria, and cholera, just to name a few. From about 1539 to the early 1700s, the death rate among the Indians was approximately 80 percent. As all tribes were affected, this severe depopulation drove many tribes to seek membership in other tribes, thus further spreading the invisible agent of death.

The Indian Removal Act

On May 28, 1830, President Andrew Jackson signed into law the Indian Removal Act. This bill was directed at the five civilized tribes: Choctaw, Chickasaw, Creek, Seminole, and Cherokee. It has been said the reason was greed on the part of Jackson as he had large land holdings in the Southeast and gold was discovered in the area. Since the Native Americans would fight the mining of gold and the destruction of nature, they had to go. Further, it may have been an appeasement to the white settlers who were moving farther west and south, assuring him of their vote in the upcoming 1832 election. Nonetheless, the tribes were to be relocated to the designated Indian territory of Oklahoma. The Choctaw were the first tribe forced to leave their land and make the overland journey on foot in 1831. The Creek and Chickasaw were next in 1832. There were many hardships with the relocation, as the Indians did not want to go and the trip had not been well planned as far as safety and necessities were concerned. To compound the problems, land grabbers and squatters were taking possession before the Indian lands were vacated. The many incidents caused the government to raucously round up the Creek and force them to move. Conditions were horrendous on the way to Oklahoma. It was bitter cold winter and there was a lack of clothing and food. Many succumbed to disease, resulting in an unimaginably high death rate. Of the approximate twenty thousand Indians who began the trip, only about fourteen thousand arrived. The Seminole rebelled and retreated to the Big Cypress Swamp in central Florida.

The most well-known removal was that of the Cherokee Indians. Their journey became known as the Trail of Tears. This was a 1,200-mile trek from their homeland in the Southeast to the Indian Territory.

Due to their resistance, the US government sent seven thousand troops to gather approximately eighteen thousand dissenters. They were captured and held in stockades. As with the other tribes, the demise of people due to disease and starvation, etc., was in the thousands. Overall, the death rate that resulted from the Indian Removal Act was 25 percent. One out of four did not survive the governmental decree.

In the late nineteenth century, the United States implemented and enforced an educational policy designed to bring the Native Americans into mainstream culture. In this effort, schools were established and the Indian children were forced to attend. The schools were managed by religious orders such as Baptist, Catholic, etc. Each tribe was assigned to a specific denomination. For example, the Creek attended the Baptist school. The US government thought the Indian children could be an asset and ready source of labor which was a needed commodity at that time. In the view of the government and religious orders, Indian teachings were considered to be a bad example and deterrent to the normal teaching environment at the schools. So, the children were removed from their homes in an effort to break Indian culture. Their hair was cut and they were forced to wear the attire of the white population. They were given English names and made to speak only English. Strict discipline, military drills, violence, and verbal abuse was common. The degradation of their culture; the humiliation and loss of their culture, self-respect, and dignity dealt a crushing blow to their spirit and led to suicide and alcoholism.

Diseases at school became a major problem as well. The object of such schools was to "Kill the Indian, save the man." Some Native Americans resisted the enforced education, hiding their children from government agents, soldiers, and missionaries. Change did not come until the mid-1930s.

It would be improper to say all boarding schools were unsuccessful and bad experiences for all of the children. There were exceptions such as Luther Standing Bear, a Brule Sioux who contributed significant literature and acted in movies. There was also Jim Thorpe, an Olympic gold medalist, professional football player, and baseball player.

Today, there are about five thousand Muskogee Indians in Georgia and Alabama. In Muskogee, Oklahoma, where they were relocated, there are now over fifty thousand living in eleven counties making up the Muskogee Nation. They have their own form of government, police force, and school system.

Tomahawk and Rattle

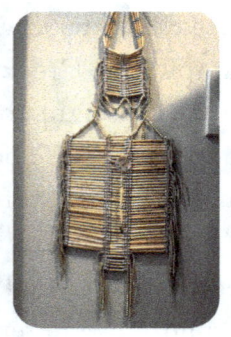

Breastplate

One Man's Spiritual Journey to Healing with Color Energy

Muskogee Ceremonial Circle

Sacred Pipe

Arrowheads, Medicine Wheel, Dreamcatcher

Pestle and Hammer Head

Basket and Indian Corn

Knife and Tomahawk

7. Initiation

My life has completely changed! My days are filled with enormous spiritual energy, both visually and intuitively, i.e., colored orbs in my room at night and around me during the day, colors flowing through my fingertips, and explicit visions. Animals, birds, reptiles, and insects participate in my prayers, walks, and meditation. As my evolvement continues, it becomes apparent a transition or metamorphosis is going to take place—the move to become a shaman, a healer. This is my calling.

I am now living on land in Georgia that was once occupied by the Muskogee, or Creek, Indians before their removal in 1832. They are still here in spirit. From time to time, Billie sees them at the nearby dam or walking through the woods. They are always present during my daily prayer ceremonies at the Sacred Circle. The Sacred Circle is a small opening in the woods beside a creek that provides solitude and serenity for my time with Spirit.

Sacred Circle

The Muskogee had an annual tradition called the Green Corn Ceremony. It was a celebration of the harvest of corn and the new year. In late summer, July or August, the new, or green, corn was ripe and full of milk. Before anyone could eat the fresh, new corn, the community prayed and fasted to put themselves in the proper mindset to receive new blessings. Rituals of cleansing, purification, forgiveness, and renewal took place. It remains an important part of the Muskogee culture today.

In honor of the Muskogee, Billie and I held a Green Corn Ceremony here on our land. We invited several people for the one-day festivity. It was well attended by not only our friends and family, but by Spirit, animals, and birds. Woodpeckers, in particular, made their presence known throughout the day. There were spiritual readings, purifications with sage, and presentations on the Muskogee history and culture. After we ate, Billie presented everyone with their own personal prayer stick that she custom made for them. She chose items from nature that spoke to each person's spiritual and personal traits. The entire event was shrouded in high spiritual energy. Everyone came away blessed and filled with a sense of peace.

Prayer Stick

In the weeks to follow, I continued to experience an increase in spiritual activity. Nature seemed to be more excited than usual. Crows, blue herons, red-tailed hawks, woodpeckers, and many other birds were eager to engage in my daily ceremonies. If they were afraid of me, it didn't show. Some would come within a few feet of me, sit, and watch as I prayed or performed my rituals of the day. Spirit was strong among us and I knew the animals were actually participating in the joyful celebrations.

One day I went to the Sacred Circle to pray. I left corn on a stone the previous day as a thanksgiving offering to the universe. To my surprise, it was still there. Every kernel. Nothing had touched it. I thought the birds or squirrels would find it immediately and it would be a quick and easy meal for them. But, there it was. Intuition told me to place my left hand over the corn and hold my spiritual stone in my right hand. I closed my eyes, cleared my mind, and concentrated on the stillness of nature that surrounded me. The stone slowly began to warm until it was almost uncomfortable to hold. At the same time, a whistling sound began to swirl above my head. I looked up and saw that it was from a bird circling around me, approximately one hundred feet in the air. The bird was familiar, but the whistling sound was not. I had never heard it before, nor have I heard it again. My eyes were drawn downward as colored orbs began to appear in front of me. They were red, purple, and gold. The colors grew in intensity as they floated around the Sacred Circle. Spiritual energy was very high and I was overcome with feelings of support, comfort, and love. I gave thanks to God and the universe for all of creation.

As I progressed on my spiritual walk, I continued to learn all I could about God and spiritualism as well the spiritual ways of the Native Americans. The role of the shaman, or medicine man, was of particular interest to me, so I read all I could get my hands on about this subject. While at the bookstore one day, I asked the woman working there for books on this topic. She brought me two books. One was *The Wind Is My Mother* by Bear Heart. I instantly knew it was brought to me by the universe. Bear Heart was a present-day medicine man in the Muskogee Nation. He was born in Oklahoma in 1918 as Marcellus Williams. He grew up in the Muskogee way, but his parents were Christian and raised him in an all-Indian Baptist church. The elders of his community selected him at an early age for training as a medicine man. Later, he earned his degree as a Baptist minister and held an honorary PhD in humanities. He strove to build a bridge between Native Americans and modern spirituality. He was a true man of God and worked tirelessly for the betterment of mankind.

The book gave me the understanding I was seeking and much more. His words were a wealth of information on Native American spiritualism. He stressed the importance of a balanced, love-centered life in service to others. Later, Bear Heart would become a part of my life in so many ways.

In August 2009, I was given a gift from Spirit. I had been praying and asking for an Indian name for myself. Since it was revealed that I was a shaman in my previous life, I wanted to assume that name in this life. At least, in my prayer life. Red-tailed hawks are frequent visitors to our home and I have always felt a connection to them. The book *Animal Speak: The Spiritual Powers of Creatures Great and Small*, by Ted Andrews, said that Indians sometimes called the red-tailed hawk "Red Eagle." It immediately felt right to me and I asked the universe if that was the name I was searching for. Spirit energy surged and I knew that I had the answer. From that day, I became Red Eagle.

My daughter and son-in-law were expecting their second child around this time. Early in the morning of August 6, I was walking along the bank of the lake on our property. A great blue heron was poised in shallow water, waiting for its next meal. Another smaller one was on the other side of the lake. Other birds began to appear. Some flew overhead while others gathered in the trees. Soon, they were everywhere and their chatter blended into a symphony of song. Finally, a woodpecker closed the wondrous show by tapping his blessing into a nearby pine tree. I was filled with joy because I knew these winged messengers of nature were anticipating good news. Spirit was sending us the gift of a healthy child. The next day, my granddaughter was born. She joined her big sister in bringing delight to our family.

The animals continued their celebration over the next few days. Deer visited frequently around the yard and the birds remained active, especially the red-tailed hawk, crows, and woodpeckers. Billie and I were discussing the increase in activity. She said that "it was a very pronounced celebration of the birth of my granddaughter and the reincarnation of her soul." As soon as she said this, the birds went silent. We both laughed. We knew this was a confirmation from the universe that it was indeed a celebration of my little granddaughter's birth. This little girl and nature's celebration of her arrival were such wonderful gifts from God.

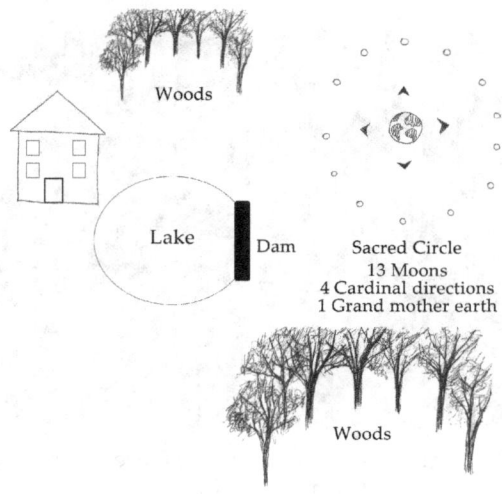

My daily ceremonies continued. I was surrounded by the happy souls of family and friends who had passed over, as well as nature in all her glory. The sun, wind, water, birds, trees, flowers joined in the celebrations. All of Creation was there to teach and to nurture.

Each day, prayers of thanksgiving and guidance opened the ceremonies followed by prayers for the needs of others, including their physical and mental healing. Music soon became an integral part of the ritual. A drum made of wood and animal hide along with a carved, wooden flute closed my prayers with peaceful melody. The serenity of the time spent with Spirit filled my soul and carried me through my days.

The birds remained very active. The hawk, crow, turkey, woodpecker, and heron often left feathers in my path. Each of them has a special influence or impact on us and brings a unique gift of Spirit. Some offer strength while others offer wisdom. I find it interesting to note that if I look for feathers, they are nowhere to be found. When I surrender to the will of Spirit, they appear in abundance. I keep every feather given to me and display them in my bedroom as a reminder of the role of nature in my life.

Prayer Center near the House
Ceremonial Circle

Flutes and Drum

Meditation is so important to spiritual growth. It has many physical and emotional benefits as well. It relieves stress, anxiety, and depression. It boosts the body's immunity to disease and increases positive energy. It promotes a general feeling of well-being and happiness. I meditate every night before going to sleep. Visions often appear to me during meditation. The face of a fox, then a wolf appeared one night. I wasn't sure what this meant so I consulted the book *Animal Speak* by Ted Andrews. The fox was sent to instruct me to trust my intuitions. The wolf was bringing my attention to the fact that my characteristics and behaviors were changing and should be culled from my consciousness. Ted Andrews wrote about animals and how they are messengers from Spirit. He wrote that animals represent various attributes or human traits. They appear to us to guide and teach us. Their behaviors are also a way they pass information to us.

Lee Hillberg

A Fox Crossed in Front of Me
Message: A new world is opening up.

During my morning prayer ceremony on September 1, 2009, I had a learning experience. A crow began calling out for a significant period of time. It was perched in a nearby tree to the north of me. After a while, it flew directly over my head and landed in a tree just to the east of me. It called over and over again until I acknowledged it. Satisfied that I received its message, it flew away. The next morning, another crow came calling. Crows continued to appear and call to me for several days. I researched crows in *Animal Speak* and *Animal Spirit Guides* by Steven Farmer. I discovered that the crows announce events that are about to take place. Something important was about to happen.

The next day, I had a reading with Carolyn Cummings. It was well attended by Spirit, family members, Indian teacher, and guides. Messages of encouragement, assurance, and guidance flowed from Spirit through Carolyn. I was asked if I had been seeing a lot of snakes. I affirmed that I had indeed seen many, especially water moccasins. Spirit advised me to consult Ted Andrews's book to determine the message the snakes were conveying. To my amazement, the snakes were delivering the news that rebirth, resurrection, initiation, and wisdom were coming my way. This was very exciting and I couldn't wait to see how it would come to be.

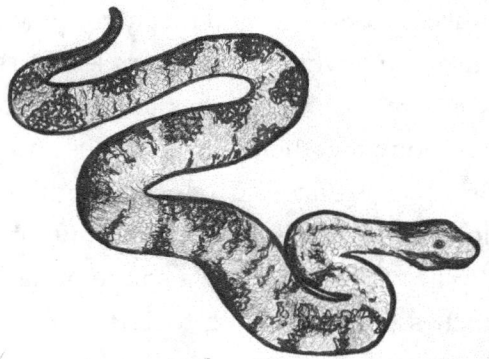

Transformation: Snake, Death & Rebirth

It wasn't long after my reading that it all started happening. My spiritual teacher, Ax, who was a shaman, or medicine man, told me I was also a shaman in a past life and that I would soon be anointed as a shaman again. I was to be prepared, as the day of initiation was approaching. So, I waited with great anticipation for the day when I would once again join the shamans, the elite group of medicine men.

Native American Man

The land I now live on was once a Muskogee/Creek Indian village. Ax revealed that it was my home in a past life. My burial site is now the place I call the Sacred Circle. The spirits of my Indian brothers and sisters surround me in this place. It is always a serene, welcoming spot where my prayers seem to soar to Spirit and peace falls as a gentle shower back to me. So, to prepare for the initiation ceremony, I gathered large stones and placed them methodically around the Sacred Circle. Spirit guided my hands as I chose the location of each stone. I stood my totem, the bear, in a prominent place at the site. It is a statue of dark-gray stone and eighteen inches tall. According to Ted Andrews in *Animal Speak*, the bear represents power, healing, and leadership.[5] It seemed appropriate for the calling of shamans. Finally, the site was ready and I would soon be initiated as Red Eagle, medicine man.

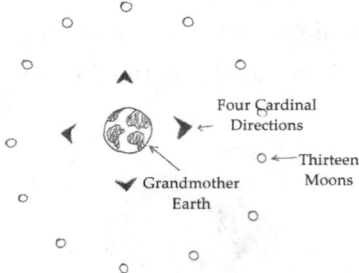

I experienced great spiritual growth during this time. Most days were filled with high spiritual energy and visions of colored orbs and animal totems. I meditated frequently and practiced chanting in anticipation of my upcoming initiation. I felt spirits all around me.

I was mowing the grass in the front yard when I saw a large feather ahead and to my right. I immediately stopped the mower. A perfect hawk feather lay on the ground. This brought me to

---

[5] Ted Andrews, *Animal Speak*.

my knees. There was no doubt that this was a message from my teacher, Ax, and spiritual guides that the initiation was near.

My Totem: A Black Bear

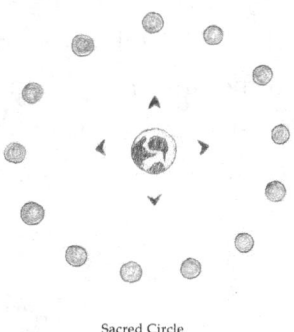

Sacred Circle
Past Life Burial Site

The next day brought spiritual lights in the form of orbs. Teal-colored orbs with red trim in various sizes danced around me. During my afternoon meditation, I fell asleep. As I began to wake, I saw the image of a bear. At the same time, the outside of my body was vibrating, head to toe. I realized I had the ability to stop the vibrations by simply telling it to stop. It immediately subsided. My room was bursting with spiritual energy. Ax had said that I would experience increased spiritual activity, and he was right. This was certainly a powerful experience, and I knew the day of initiation was not far away.

October 1, 2009, was a beautiful day. The temperature was in the midfifties, there was no wind, the sky was clear, and there was a slight mist rising from the lake. There were five wild turkeys walking across the yard toward the lake. I walked to the garage. As I approached it, I closed my eyes and saw Indian spirit lights. They were the teal orbs with red trim that I had previously seen in my room. They moved from the bottom of my vision to the top. Was this a message that perhaps this was initiation day? I was not sure, so I decided to go for a walk in the woods.

Near the lake, a red-tailed hawk called from the northeast. It continued calling for a moment then flew over the trees and turned in the direction of the Sacred Circle. I knew then that this was the day. So, I got my spiritual healing stone and green candle and went to the Sacred Circle. With my stone in hand, I offered a prayer to connect with the universe. I then lit the candle and sat inside the circle. Immediately the sound of birds, geese, crows, and woodpeckers filled the air.

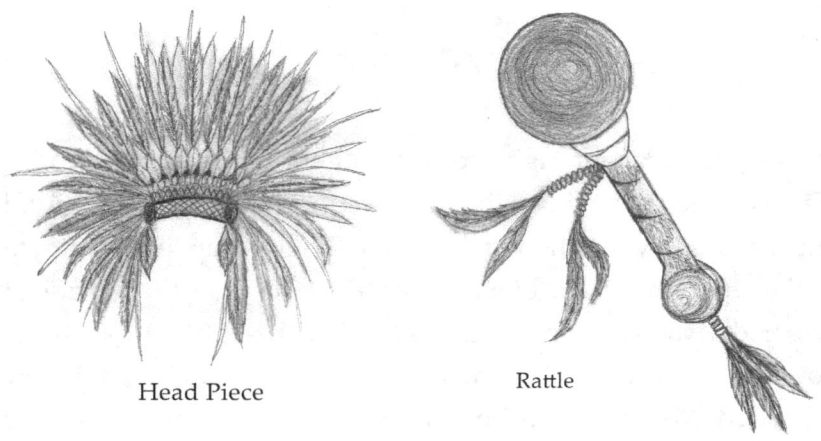

Head Piece   Rattle

Bear Skin

The initiation began with visions of the color gold and a hawk calling out several times. A copper color appeared near the candle. I felt water drops on my head. Suddenly, all I could see was very bright gold with high spiritual energy. This energy entered my body and I began to vibrate and shake. It lasted a few moments, then stopped. Everything was quiet. Soon, the vibrations began again. In total, there were three sets of vibrations, each lasting a short period of time. They were each accompanied by the water droplets falling on my head and the sound of the birds in the trees. All the while, the entire area was consumed in an energy that felt as if it had been electrically charged. At some point, I stood and began chanting and dancing, turning clockwise. The dancing slowed and I settled into the circle once again. At that point, I felt the presence of Bear Heart. His spirit was strong and I felt the metaphysical offering of his ceremonial rattle. He then placed his headpiece upon my head and his bearskin wrap around my shoulders. I humbly accepted each one. I followed with a prayer of thanks to God the Creator, Bear Heart, Ax, my spirit guides, and all who were gathered at my initiation.

I made a special offering to God in appreciation for the opportunity He had bestowed upon me. I also dedicated myself fully to serving humbly, fearlessly, and with honor in this journey as a shaman. Facing the four cardinal directions of north, south, east, and west, I vowed to fill the honored role with love, honesty, faith, and charity. At this time, the area went very quiet with no birds, no hawk, no woodpecker. Without question, the ceremony had ended. I was humbled and grateful to the point of feeling weak. I dried the tears of joy from my eyes and returned to the house to tell Billie of this wondrous event.

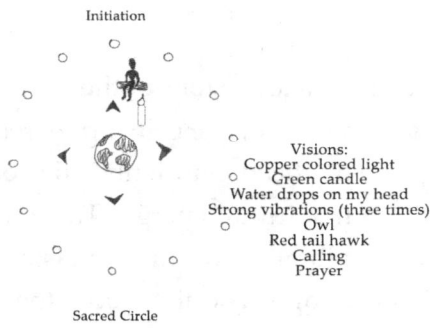

I had been advised by Bear Heart, after the ceremony, to eat strawberries. Later that day, I took some to the ceremonial site. I also took my sacred stone, flute, and drum with me. I ate the strawberries then performed a quiet celebration of gratefulness. Immediately, I received a vision of a red beetle. It was walking around on my hand. This was a message from Bear Heart. The beetle represents metamorphosis or resurrection, so it seemed highly appropriate that he would send this insect to me now.

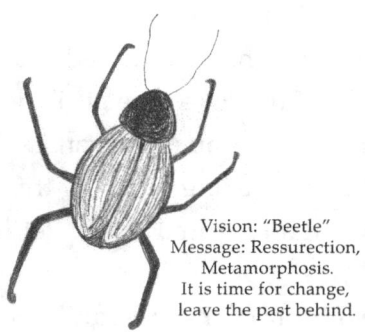

Vision: "Beetle"
Message: Ressurection, Metamorphosis.
It is time for change, leave the past behind.

In the days following the shaman initiation, I spent a lot of time meditating. The colors purple, gold, yellow, and blue appeared around me, over and over again. The colors would often open and close at the center, much like a flower blooming. Birds, including an eagle and red-tailed hawk, were always near and called out to me. Occasionally, the hawk would fly directly over my head. Several times, I found the hawk's feathers on my path. The hawk is a messenger of the spirit world, and the feathers were tokens of encouragement. If a hawk visits, there will be an important message in the near future. Hawks also bring great visionary power. The hawk was telling me to focus on my new vocation and be aware that more gifts from Spirit were on the way.

I began fasting and performing purification rituals. I burned dried sage to cleanse my soul and rid the area of any unwanted or negative energy. My prayers included thanksgiving and gratitude to God for His gifts of the universe and family.

Meditation continued daily. I received visions of animal spirits such as the bear, horse, and cougar. They moved so fast in the visions that I could barely keep up. It seemed to me that the speed of the animals matched the high level of spiritual energy and growth I was experiencing at the time.

In the book *The Wind Is My Mother*, Bear Heart writes that one does not ask to be a shaman or medicine man. You must be invited by the elders of the tribe. The attributes are instinctive, or inborn, and the individual must lead an exemplary life. Never had I even thought about being a part of this elite group. It was not something that I had aspired to be. Yet here I was a newly initiated shaman.

This was the beginning of an awesome journey. God would use me to deliver His love and healing to those who so desperately need them. He will no doubt guide my every step and lead me down this path. I was humbled beyond belief.

Ceremonial Attire: Headdress and Sacred Pipe

Thus far, my journey had been filled with learning through spirit guides and study. The simple day-to-day events of walking through the woods, interacting with nature, and talking with Billie were just a few of the ways I grew in Spirit. Visions, prayers, dreams, colored orbs, reading, and studying all contributed to my growth.

During my daily ceremonies, I tried to be observant of details of the orbs I saw in my visions. I recorded, in journals, the number, colors, direction, and speed of their movement. Spirit does nothing by chance, so I did not omit anything I saw. Even though I may not understand the meaning of a vision immediately, the explanation would surely be apparent later.

8. It's Time

A new level of existence has opened up to me—healing with color.

My life was changing. It was changing at such a high rate of speed that it could only be supernatural. During a reading with Carolyn Cummings, my teacher, Ax, came in. He conveyed the message that my spiritual transformation would be "fast and furious." That was a perfect description of what I was feeling. I was being fine-tuned and it was being done quickly.

This was an amazing transformation, a conversion, a new level of existence. The message I received through Carolyn was that it was now time to begin a ministry of healing using colors given by God, our Creator. All healing comes from God, and He now wanted to use me as His instrument. I was willing and ready to serve Him in that way. I vowed to be faithful and unswerving on this mission.

I had been seeing colored orbs for a while now. Some were only one color, while others were multicolored. The significance of the color wasn't always obvious, although at times, I intuitively knew their meanings. I guess intuition is part of the gift I've been given. Through prayer and research, the power of each color has been revealed and I have learned how to apply them to various health issues.

In the days following my shaman initiation, I spent a lot of time meditating. The colors purple, gold, yellow, and blue appeared around me, over and over again. The colors would often open and close at the center, much like a flower blooming. Birds, including an eagle and red-tailed hawk, were always near and called out to me. Occasionally, the hawk would fly directly over my head. Several times, I found the hawk's feathers on my path. The hawk is a messenger of the spirit world and the feathers were tokens of encouragement. If a hawk visits, there will be an important message in the near future. Hawks also bring great visionary power. The hawk was telling me to focus on my new vocation and be aware that more gifts from Spirit were on the way.

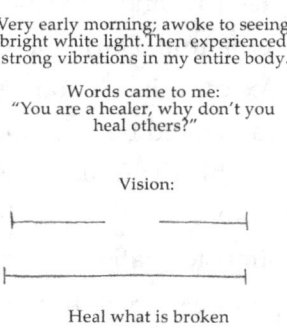

Very early morning; awoke to seeing bright white light. Then experienced strong vibrations in my entire body.

Words came to me:
"You are a healer, why don't you heal others?"

Vision:

Heal what is broken

I began fasting and performing purification rituals. I burned dried sage to cleanse my soul and rid the area of any unwanted or negative energy. Prayers included thanksgiving and gratitude to God for His gifts of the universe and family.

My journey had been filled with learning through spirit guides and study. The simple day-to-day events of walking through the woods, interacting with nature, and talking with Billie were just a few of the ways I grew in Spirit. Visions, prayers, dreams, and colored orbs all contributed in inspiring me to new heights of spiritual awakening.

Billie and I attended a Muskogee and Seminole powwow in Florida that October. It was another incredible learning experience. The descendants of these two great Indian nations convened to celebrate their heritage and share it with their children. They performed authentic traditional dances and music of their tribes. Men, women, and children dressed in the regalia of their ancestors and danced to the deep, resonating beats of the rawhide-covered drums. Men wore buckskin pants and ribbon shirts. The women wore magnificent buckskin dresses with beaded moccasins.

Later, they paid special tribute to the veterans of their communities. They marched out on the field. First the flag bearers, then the staff bearers. Finally, drums beat a cadence as the veterans marched onto the field, four deep.

Shaman Headdress Gifted to Me by Jerry Lang

We watched in awe as the festivities progressed into the evening. Billie, overcome with compassion for what the Native Americans had endured over the years and for their struggle to keep their heritage alive, broke down into tears. The entire event filled us with reverence and love for these people.

Before we left the powwow, I bought a handmade Indian flute and drum. They are very special to me and I continue to play them in my daily ceremonies. But the most special token of that day, aside from the memories, was a gift from Jerry Lang, a Muskogee medicine man. I met him early in the day and we became fast friends. I learned that Bear Heart had been one of his teachers. It was a great privilege to talk to someone who actually knew Bear Heart and could relay his teachings firsthand. We talked about Bear Heart, our own experiences, and the responsibilities of being medicine men. To my surprise, he presented me with his own shaman headpiece. It is a cap covered with black, cotton material that is folded around the side. Tiny beige stars scatter throughout and two taupe-colored ostrich feathers rise from the right side. Each time I wear this headpiece, I am reminded of my friend and fellow shaman, Jerry Lang. I am honored and proud to share this walk with him.

Me with Jerry Lang

9. The Power of Color

Color is all around us. It affects our moods. We decorate our homes and ourselves with color. We are awed and moved by colors in nature. I have been guided to understand the effects and spiritual energy directly related to color in health and healing.

Color affects everyone and is connected to all aspects of our lives. We use color to describe our physical health, our emotional state, attitude, and our spiritual encounters. Color is vibrational energy, and those vibrations exist in all objects as well as animals, people, and the atmosphere. Color is everywhere.

Each color has its own unique effect and its own vibrational energy which can be directed to healing and balancing one's body, spirit, and mind. Understanding that different frequencies of light, appearing as color, will affect different energies of the body is helpful when selecting and applying color in healing. Healing with color works in harmony with traditional medicine. Color, on the other hand, is not prescriptive and is not designed to replace traditional medicine. It is, however, a means which allows you to participate more personally in your own health and healing process.

Light is the electromagnetic energy produced by the sun. Everything we see is reflected light. The atoms of light are moving, literally vibrating, at different speeds which causes wavelengths to be longer or shorter. The slower the vibration, the longer the wavelength and the less energy. Faster-vibrating atoms cause shorter wavelengths and more energy. Blue or green, for instance, is a cool color. The wavelength is long, as there is not as much energy being emitted. The faster-vibrating atoms cause shorter wavelengths and emit warmer colors such as yellow or violet.

Selecting the appropriate color is key to the most effective healing. It is a trial-and-error process. With practice and experience, you will find that it becomes second nature. There are some things, however, that I find to be helpful. As mentioned earlier, basic knowledge of chakras and the ability to read auras is essential. It is important to perform a chakra assessment by taking note of different conditions, physical or otherwise, that are affecting the individual at the time. Determine the color or colors which will be used for therapy through the use of a dowsing rod or pendulum. These two instruments deliver energy, through color, required to heal a specific health condition. Kinesiology, or testing muscle groups, gives us tangible feedback about health as well. Also, Spirit will lead and inspire you, so do not ignore your intuition.

Ted Andrews wrote a book, *How to Heal with Color*. I learned a tremendous amount from him and still refer to his book as needed. Ted Andrews has been a tremendous source of support to me, not only from his book, but also through his spiritual guidance since his passing in 2009. I refer to him frequently and appreciate all he has taught me.

In *How to Heal with Color*, Ted Andrews talks about the colors and combinations of colors in aiding certain conditions. As one can imagine, each individual will be different and you may find that the same color will not work for everyone. You may have to experiment with various shades to find the one that works best. The following is a summary of Ted Andrews's identification of colors and their effects.

White, according to Ted, contains the entire light spectrum. It is a cleansing, purifying color and has strengthening qualities.

One can be confident in beginning and ending healing sessions with white, as it stabilizes the body's energy systems and gives them a boost. It can also be used in conjunction with other colors to increase their effect.

Black is confusing to a lot of people. However, it is similar to white in that it also contains the entire color spectrum. Black has protective qualities and can be a calming color to those who may be sensitive or need grounding. It can stimulate and strengthen the feminine energies. Do not be afraid to use it if you feel that it is necessary, but never by itself. Always pair it with other colors. Be careful not to overuse it, as it can cause depression or accelerate other mental conditions. When used with white, black has a balancing effect. If an individual seems to be out of control or out of touch with reality, you can apply black and white in order to stabilize the emotional or psychological state.

Red stimulates and energizes the base chakras. It can raise the temperature of the body and energize the blood. It can be used to aid in mucus ailments such as a cold by speeding up the flow of fluid to relieve congestion. The same is true of poor circulation. Applying red to the area will increase blood flow. Red can stimulate the passions such as love, sex, courage, and hatred. On the other hand, high blood pressure can indicate that there is too much red in the system.

Orange dominates the second chakra center. This color is tied to our emotional and muscular systems. It arouses joy and wisdom. Depression and other emotional disorders can benefit from orange. It can also be used to aid in the healing of the spleen, pancreas, stomach, intestines, and the adrenals. Basically, orange is a good color for the digestive system because it revitalizes the body and promotes food absorption. Too much orange can affect the nerves and should be balanced with blue-greens.

Yellow is found in the solar plexus chakra. It, also, can relieve depression. Yellow stimulates the mental facilities and enthusiasm for life. If an individual struggles with a lack of confidence or optimism, yellow can be helpful. It is another color that can relieve symptoms associated with digestive disorders. It can help balance the gastrointestinal tract and elimination system.

Green affects the heart chakra. It is all around us on this earth and throughout nature. It calms, balances our energies, and increases our sensitivities and compassion. It soothes the nervous system. Green lifts our faith, brings hope, and inspires peace. It can settle anxieties and encourage rest. Cardiac conditions, as well as high blood pressure, respond to green. Individuals feeling fatigue respond to green. Since it stimulates growth, it should never be used on any condition that involves malignant tumors or cancer.

Blue is found in the throat chakra. It is a relaxing and soothing color. It awakens intuition and artistic expression. Because of its cooling nature, blue is one of the most effective colors used for childhood diseases. Asthma, chicken pox, jaundice, and rheumatism are eased by the application of blue. Headaches are commonly relieved by blue. It is the primary color used for high blood pressure and throat conditions. It can be advantageous to combine blue with warmer colors in the red-orange shades.

Indigo is found in the brow chakra. It is a powerful agent for healing both the physical and spiritual aspects of an individual. Indigo can bring one to a deeper level of consciousness when used during meditation. It strengthens the endocrine system and purifies the blood. It aids in detoxifying the body. Indigo balances the hemispheres of the brain. It can be used in treating sinuses, eyes, ears, nose, and mouth as well as the lungs. It has a sedative effect which is helpful in removing obsessions. But the sedative effect can cause depression if too much indigo is used.

Violet is in the crown chakra. It balances the physical and spiritual energies of the body and governs the skeletal system.

Along with its antiseptic qualities, violet can also be used to strengthen the body's ability to process minerals. Violet that tends toward blue is good at easing arthritis. Its cleansing and purifying property also makes it excellent for use in cancer treatment. Psychologically, violet stimulates inspiration and increases humility. It is a vehicle for dream activity and opening ourselves up to our past lives.

Pink is a motivational color that lifts your spirits. It inspires compassion, love, and purity. It is comforting and helps us to heal from episodes of anger and neglect. Pink facilitates an increase in immunity.

Lemon, which contains a hint of green in its spectrum, stimulates the brain. It cleanses the body by bringing toxins to the surface where they can be removed.

Gold is another color that stimulates the immune system. It raises the individual's ability to aid in their own healing. One must be enthusiastic about maintaining their health, and gold is great at bringing about that zest for life.

Royal blue processes oxygen and clears the mind. It is extremely antiseptic and can help to rid the body of physical ailments.

Aqua is also a cooling color. Fever and other inflammations can be diminished from the application of aqua.

Turquoise is another color that cools and soothes. Since it is a combination of green and blue, it is a good choice when you want to restore or purify the system. Skin conditions, earaches, and acute pain respond well to turquoise.

Purple can be used to soothe and decrease inflammation. The blue-purple shade is effective at shrinking tumors such as cancer. It has high vibrational energy, so it should be used sparingly. In excess, it can aggravate depression.

Silver and gray can be used in the same way white is used. Alone, silver and gray can help one to discover the cause or source of an ailment. They also help in the discovery and application of creativity and intuition. Used in combination with other colors, they amplify the effect of the other color used.

Brown can be used to bring someone "back down to earth." When an individual has lost sight of reality or needs to implore common sense, brown can be an effective color to use. It is very successful in treating emotional and mental conditions.

Once you have identified the ailment and decided on the color to be used, you must now apply the color to the individual. There are several ways this can be done. You can project a color through your hands into the area of the body that is in need of balance. This is called etheric touch. It is a method of using the hands to direct energies, human and spiritual, to help heal. You may have heard the expression, "laying of hands" used in spiritual ceremonies. Energy follows thought. As we concentrate on a certain color, the energy signal is sent to the hands and projected out. Our hands are strong points of sensitivity and we do have minor chakra centers in them. We are able to radiate energy outward from our hands into another body. Actual contact is not necessary, although it can sometimes enhance the healing process. This form of healing has always been considered a more spiritual form of healing. As you breathe, you pull energy down through your own body and send, or radiate, it out of your hands to heal and balance the individual. The energy takes on the frequency of your thoughts and extends to the other person. As you concentrate on the color chosen, the frequency of that color is absorbed by the person being treated. The amazing thing about this type of healing is that it can be done in person or from a distance (distance healing). To begin, you simply close your eyes and imagine the color on the palm of your hands. Place your hands slightly above the body, moving slowly back and forth over the afflicted area. Continue for a few moments, concentrating on the color in your mind. Have the individual you are helping also visualize the color in their mind. There is no set time period for application. You will become a good judge of time as you grow in experience.

Headaches are a common ailment. They are also easily managed with color. You can treat your own headache by using the etheric touch method. Close your eyes and imagine the color blue, pale blue, or green. If this is difficult for you, you can focus on a cloth or object of one of these colors. They are very effective for headaches due to their calming, soothing effect. Concentrate on the color while holding the palms of your hands close to your head. You will feel the energy from your hands as you slowly move them around your head and face. Take deep breaths and relax. The pain will soon dissipate and you will feel relief.

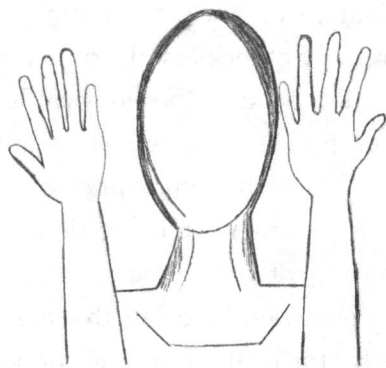

Healing a Headache with Color Energy

Other methods of applying color are easy and a matter of choice by you or the individual being treated. One is to lay colored cloth swatches to the chakra or area of the body needing treatment. You can also place colored candles around the individual in order to assist in the healing session. A slide of color can be projected for visualization. If the individual wishes, they can drink water that has been colored the appropriate color. These are all methods that can be implemented to transfer the energy of the color to the body.

As mentioned earlier, healing does not have to be done in person. It can be accomplished from a distance. Long-distance healing is a very effective method to assist those who cannot be present for a healing ceremony. This is similar to sending prayers to others who are not present. It is not a new concept; in fact, it has been practiced throughout the ages. It is based on the premise that energy is everywhere and in various forms. The human body is an energy system and works together with the energy of the universe. Our energy affects that of the universe and vice versa. In distance healing, we transcend time and space. Our focus is on controlling our mind and allowing the energy of the color to connect with the individual at the receiving end.

Whenever we perform a distance healing, it is important to have a clear, defined identity of the person being healed. It helps to have a picture, address, or other personal object of the individual to establish a connection beyond the physical level. First, make sure you are clear on the ailment or imbalance that needs to be addressed. Then, decide which method and color will be used.

Any time I do in-person healing sessions, I must have a thorough understanding of the ailment, pain, location of the imbalance, etc. Spirit provides the colors that are to be used, but I still need to prepare for the healing through prayer, thought, and research.

Be sure to open and close each session with prayer. Affirm with any healing, especially long-distance healing, that the healing manifest "for the good of all according to the free will of all." We do not have the right to intrude upon the free will of others. Also, it is very important to balance the chakras before and at the end of each session.

My first distance healing involved a young man whom I had been doing healing prayers for over several weeks. He suffered from a consistent, nagging cough that would not go away. His mother and grandmother were concerned and feared the cough was an indication of serious health issues. His grandmother asked that I perform a distance healing on him, and she provided a picture of the boy. During my morning ceremony the next day, I asked Spirit to tell me when the healing session should take place. Later that morning, I was working in the garage when I heard a bird call out in a very sharp, loud cry. As I looked out, a red-tailed hawk flew close and low to the ground in a south-southwest direction. I knew that I was to go to the Sacred Circle and perform the ceremony. I took the picture I had been given, along with his name and address, and went to the site. I held the picture and my spiritual stone in my hands and asked God for the healing of this young man. At first, I concentrated on the picture of the boy, sending white crystal energy throughout his crown chakra. White would stabilize and boost his body's energy systems. Then, I moved to his throat because this was the central area that needed healing. At that time, I saw a dark-blue-to-purple color appear on his throat. The color remained on his throat and face for two to three minutes. Purple can signify mental imbalances. The appearance of dark blue and purple told me that this was most likely the case. I was confident that the problem was of an emotional origin, not physiological. I proceeded to balance the other chakras, then finished with prayers of thanksgiving to God and the universe.

This young man sought the help of a mental health professional, and the cough dissipated. His family was relieved that the issue was not life threatening and could be managed with proper care.

Chakras

The human body must have a balance in energy to maintain health, or homeostasis. Illness is the result of imbalance, whether it is physical or mental. The body works as a whole. Since all body systems rely on each other for health, an imbalance of either the mental or physical state can cause illness in the other. In order to return to normal, a healthy energy level must be regained. This is where color comes into play.

The human body is an energy system divided into centers called chakras. The chakras are pure energy fields, neither physical nor anatomical. However, they do influence our cells, organs, and the entire endocrine system. They are the center of psychic energy and affect our thoughts and feelings. There are seven main chakras, and many secondary chakras, that govern the emotional, physical, and spiritual well-being of the human body. Located near the spinal column, each chakra gives and receives its own unique spiritual energy. They are the primary mediators of all energy coming into and radiating from the body, acting like little suns. They link the subtle energy fields surrounding the body to the activities of the body itself. The chakras take energy from the environment; from nature, including the sun and planets; and from other people. Each deals with a specific function of the body and spirit. But each must be opened, or activated, to release its full potential.

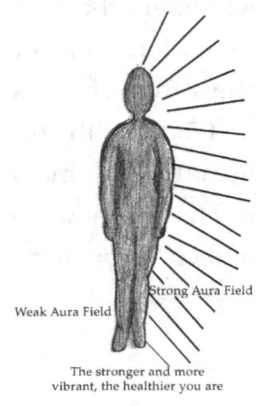

Weak Aura Field   Strong Aura Field

The stronger and more vibrant, the healthier you are

The vibrational energy released by the chakras is distributed throughout the body by the nervous and circulatory systems. Sound, color, aromatherapy, and naturopathic remedies can all be used to improve circulation, thereby promoting well-being.

For the purpose of this writing, we will only focus on the seven main chakras and the colors associated with each.

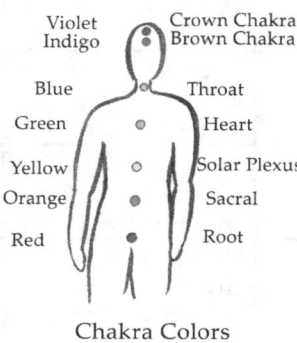

Chakra Colors

Chakra therapy is the art of healing with energy. Its purpose is to balance and open each chakra, resulting in holistic healing. It is only natural that color would be used in this practice. Individual chakras and the organs related to them respond to specific colors. Color is applied to the area of the body where imbalance occurs. The color energy produces a vibration within the chakra that is sent to the spine. The spine then sends the vibrational energy to the organ or system needing balance.

The seven chakras and their corresponding colors are as follows:

Chakra	Color	Color Application
Crown	Violet	Underactive: apply violet to provide stimulate the chakra. Overactive: apply yellow followed by a small of violet.
Brow	Indigo	Underactive: apply indigo to stimulate the chakra. Overactive: soft orange or peach followed by small dose of indigo.
Throat	Blue	Underactive: apply blue to stimulate the chakra. Overactive: orange followed by a small dose of blue.
Heart	Green	Underactive: apply green to stimulate the chakra. Overactive: green followed by pink or soft red.
Solar Plexus	Yellow	Underactive: apply yellow to stimulate the chakra. Overactive: violet or purple followed by yellow.
Sacral	Orange	Underactive: apply orange to stimulate the chakra. Overactive: blue followed by a small dose of orange.
Root	Red	Underactive: Apply red to stimulate the chakra. Overactive: green followed by a small dose of red.

There are basic steps to follow in chakra therapy. First, you must determine which chakra or chakras are out of balance. This is accomplished by assessing the physical or mental condition of the individual. Next, you must decide if the chakra is overactive or underactive. This is not difficult, as the overactive will present as inflammation, agitation, or hypersensitivity. The opposite is true for the underactive. It will appear sluggish, slow, or depressed. You would then apply the appropriate color to the chakra using any of the methods discussed in the chapter on healing with color. It is beneficial to follow this with a ten- or fifteen-second balance treatment to each of the seven chakras, working from the base, or root chakra, to the crown chakra.

For example, the root, or base chakra is located at the end of the spine. It is the center of our life force. If it is congested, or underactive, it can cause fatigue, anemia, or the inability to perform at full capacity. By applying the color red, the congested chakra is stimulated and returns to normal activity. On the other hand, if the chakra is overstimulated, it can cause high blood pressure or aggression. Applying the color green will calm and soothe the chakra. This can be done with each chakra, using the colors described above.

There are books written on the use of color in healing. One of them, *How to Heal with Color,* by Ted Andrews, is a tremendous tool that I have used often. His work aided me in the early stages of my journey and continues to be of help to me today.

Since his passing in 2009, Ted Andrews's spirit is strong and is a frequent visitor and guide in my daily ceremonies. Carolyn Cummings told me, during a reading in January 2011, that Ted came in and said he was my sponsor and would carry a guiding light for me throughout my life. According to Ted, I am a healer because my heart is humble. He said the truly good healers, and he included me in that category, show humility with nature, animals, and color. I am inspired by his constant support and will always welcome the wisdom he lends from the other side.

The Aura

The human aura is an energy field that surrounds the physical body. It comes from within and extends outward in an elliptical pattern around the person. The healthier the body, the farther the aura extends. The average aura extends as much as eight to ten feet.

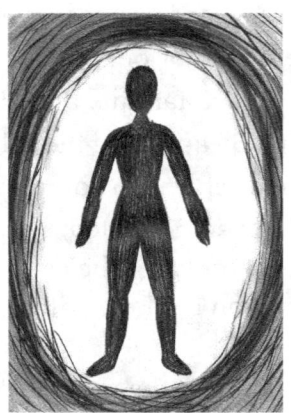

The Human Aura
The aura surrounds the physical body.
Elliptical shape, size, colors and clarity
are indications about our health.

The aura reflects the physical, emotional, and spiritual aspects of the individual. Of course, it is in color, and the clarity, size, and shape of the color all provide information about the well-being of that person. It stands to reason that the aura would be used as a diagnostic tool in healing. Seeing the aura is the easy part. Interpreting the aura can be the difficult part because it can change throughout the day. It is affected by one's experiences and emotions, which affect the energy of the body. Both internal and external energy fields come into play. We are one with nature, so the very presence of the plants and animals in our lives can interact with and transform our own energy field. This, in turn, affects the colors of the aura.

Native Americans have traditionally used totems to connect and align with nature. This strengthens the forces between the human body and its surroundings. The body absorbs the external energy, increasing the energy of the individual. For example, a common form of healing is to send someone suffering from an illness to the ocean. The ocean environment has the four basic elements of life. There is fire from the sun, air from the ocean breeze, earth from the land, and water from the ocean itself. Think of the healing nature of water alone. The simple act of soaking in a tub of water has a tremendous rejuvenating effect on the body.

Combine the cleansing and calming power of water with other elements of nature, including color, and the body returns to the natural state of balance.

All elements in nature strive for balance. The human body instinctively works to maintain balance physically, mentally, and spiritually. The aura can be used to identify areas of the body that are out of balance and need healing or improvements in daily health.

If there is a lack of symmetry in the radiant line of energy, there is an indication of weakness or disease somewhere in the physical body. This shows as a distortion, and it will usually be seen in the area of the body where the affliction exists.

Learning to See the Aura

Since the aura is a physical condition, not a metaphysical condition, anyone can learn to see it. It can be seen in two ways: intuitively or objectively. Either way is equally effective. The key, or trick, is to interpret it correctly. If the person is not present, the intuitive reading is done by relaxing with eyes closed and visualizing the person in your mind. Ask your intuitive self to present the primary colors of that individual's aura. Then, ask if there are any other colors and where are they located. What do these colors tell you about the individual's physical, emotional, mental, and spiritual level? In my experiences, the intuitive perceptions are as close to accurate as the objective or physical perceptions. Use your own judgment. If you need tangible awareness, it is always acceptable to use the objective method. Over time, you will become confident in your abilities and the accuracy of your own readings.

Practice seeing auras. On a warm, clear day, look up to the trees and let your eyes run from the base of a tree to the top. Let your eyes focus on the treetops and tree line against the blue sky. Relax and take in as much of the blue sky as possible. Soon, you will become aware of a soft haze, lighter than the sky, that follows the horizontal outline of treetops.

Another exercise that is useful in learning to see auras is to place your hand against a white backdrop. Focus on your hand. Once again, you will notice a light, soft haze appearing around your hand and fingers. It is possible that you see more than one color.

Seeing the Aura of Others

After you have become comfortable and can see the aura of trees and your own hand, have someone stand against a light-colored wall. Clear the area around them on the wall so that there is an adequate amount of empty space on the wall surrounding the individual. Dim the lights and stand eight to ten feet away. Make sure you can see the person from their head to their toes. Focus on the forehead and, moving your eyes in a clockwise direction, circle the person several times. This will condition your eyes and prepare them to see the aura. Return your focus to the forehead then move to the top of the head. Hold your focus for fifteen to thirty seconds. Slowly shift your focus to a wide area that encompasses the body. Hold this "soft" focus until you see the head and shoulders begin to stand out. Repeat these steps as necessary. It can be helpful to sketch the aura and the positions of colors you observe. Since memory can fade, you will have this sketch to refer to as you attempt to read and interpret the meaning.

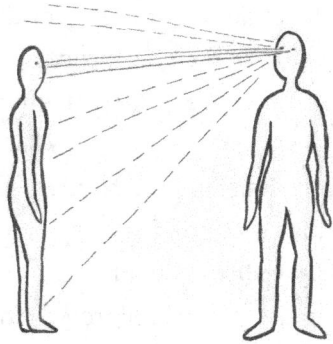
Seeing the Aura of Others

The Meaning of Colors in the Aura

Interpreting the meaning of colors in the aura is in keeping with healing with colors. Obviously, one has to know what the colors represent in order to apply healing when an infliction or unhealthy condition is present. As discussed earlier, different colors emit different amounts of energy. They reflect different attitudes, moods, and energy patterns. As you practice reading auras and healing with color, there are some guidelines to keep in mind. First of all, colors closest to the human body usually reflect physical conditions and energies. The outer colors reflect emotional, mental, and spiritual energies. The clearer and more pastel colors are, the better. Muddy and thick colors reflect imbalances or possible problems in the area to which the colors are associated. Dark colors that are bright, or vivid, can indicate high energy. This is not necessarily bad. As you learn more about colors and their energies, it will become easier to interpret the intensity of certain colors. Often, there is more than one color in the aura. Practice will aid you in deciphering the interactions and combinations of colors. It is important to remember that you should not make judgments about the information you receive. Use your intuition in interpreting what you see but be careful that your personal thoughts or feelings do not influence the reading. Again, remember the aura can change frequently and that the color and its clarity, as well as location of the color, can indicate different things. A person's aura will change with their emotions, physical, and emotional states.

So, practice and be persistent, but don't be discouraged if results are not coming quickly. As with anything worth pursuing, it takes time. The rewards are worth the wait.

Once you have read and interpreted the aura, discuss the information with the individual and get his or her feedback. Care must be taken in communicating the reading with them. Since there are so many variables to take into account such as location, intensity, shades, etc. of the colors of the aura, the feedback from the individual becomes integral in a proper assessment of the reading. At the same time, trust your own intuition and align yourself with the higher forces of life. Trust your "Higher Self"!

It is very important to note that only a medical doctor is authorized to diagnose, prescribe, or recommend treatment of disease. However, your assessment of the aura may be beneficial to leading that person on the right path to health.

As stated earlier, primary colors are typically seen in the aura. Other colors such as green, violet, purple, gold, pink, brown, black, and white can also appear. In the book *The Meaning of Colors in the Aura*, the author, Ted Andrews, describes the meaning of many colors. Green represents "sensitivity and growing compassion." It can show growth, sympathy, and calm. "It is a color of abundance, strength, and friendliness." When the green becomes darker, or muddy, it could indicate uncertainty, self-doubt, or mistrust.

Blue is a color frequently seen in the aura. It represents calm or peace. It also indicates devotion and truth. Lighter shades of blue reflect good intuition and imagination. Darker shades could mean loneliness. Deeper shades can indicate levels of devotion, while royal blue can tell a person whether or not he or she has found their life work. Muddy shades of blue indicate worry, fear, or even oversensitivity.

Purple and violet are colors that represent the blending of the heart and mind or the physical with the spiritual. They can indicate independence and intuition as well as the ability to be practical and worldly. Red-purple indicates great passion or strong will. Darker or muddy shades reflect the need to overcome something. They can also indicate the individual is feeling misunderstood or needs sympathy.

Pink presents as a color of love, compassion, and purity. It is known to reflect joy, comfort, and a sense of companionship. In the aura, it can mean that the person loves art and beauty or is modest or quiet. The muddier shades can represent immaturity. It also can indicate that the individual has found new love or a new outlook on life.

Gold expresses personal power or spiritual growth. If gold is seen, it is likely that the individual is experiencing new levels of harmony or high devotion. He or she may be going through a time of revitalization. The muddy shades of gold can reveal that the person is not clear on a path to take or that a process of awakening higher inspiration has not been fully developed.

If white appears, if reflects truth and purity. The individual is experiencing cleansing and purifying. It could also indicate an awakening of greater creativity.

The color gray reflects initiation. It can reveal that the person is uncovering innate abilities. If the color leans toward silver, the person may be awakening feminine energies such as illumination, intuition, and creative imagination. If the gray is darker, it can reflect physical imbalances, particularly when it is seen on specific areas of the body. Sometimes, gray indicates a person who is secretive or a loner.

The earth is represented in the color brown and often appears in the aura. If it appears above the head or around the feet, it can mean new growth. New roots are being established and the person has a desire to accomplish something in his or her life. Brown can also reflect industry and organization. If, however, brown is across the face or touching the head, it may reflect a need for discrimination. In the chakra areas, it can indicate that those centers need cleansing. In other words, those areas are clogged. Feedback from the individual is particularly important with the color brown. It can indicate physical problems, but it is essential to talk with the individual before jumping to that conclusion.

Black can be the most confusing color to interpret. Some people fear black, thinking it indicates death or disease. This is not necessarily true. In most cases, it represents protection. The individual is being shielded from outside energies. In the aura, it may mean that the person is protecting himself. Or, it can indicate the person has secrets. This is not necessarily a bad thing. However, black can also reflect imbalances. Location provides clues to whether or not black represents protection or imbalance. If it appears in the outer edges of the aura, it can mean holes in the auric field. Causes of this can be extreme but, again, do not jump to conclusions should this show up while reading the aura.

There are other effects that show when reading auras. Sometimes "silver twinkies," or soft, twinkling lights are seen. They are usually silver and sparkle. Typically, they reflect fertility or creativity. If they appear around women, it could mean pregnancy, but not necessarily. However, they are most often seen around women who are pregnant or who have given birth within the past six to nine months.

10. Nature's Magic

Elves, fairies, and devas are all part of nature's magic. And yes, I believe in magic.

Nature is the most powerful realm of spirituality and magic upon the earth. It is the source and origin of energies and great spirits. Within nature are found most of life's lessons and most of life's answers as well. There are teachings about life, death, and rebirth. Nature is an endless source of guidance in our walk on Mother Earth. It provides help in problem solving, accomplishing tasks, building respect, encouragement, and trust. It opens us to our greatest possibilities and dreams. It holds wonderful magic and is our greatest guide. Through nature, we can observe, firsthand, the circle of life, growth, support, giving, and receiving. Tearing down the old and building up the new.

We must recognize that we are a part of nature, not a ruler or lord of it. We must learn to understand the messages of nature as it speaks to us in many different ways. We have a stewardship role with the natural world. Plants and animals are part of us. They are companions, healers, teachers, and spirit messengers. At times, they need protection and we are here to provide that. As such, we need to respect, protect, and honor all of nature as a family member.

Native Americans have always recognized that they are a part of nature and given due respect to her. To them, everything is a gift of the earth and is to be held sacred.

There are wonderful benefits in working with nature. The reward of being a steward is a closer walk with the divine. We are able to quiet ourselves, meditate, and become intuitive, which allows us to experience a sharpening of the senses. Taking care of our environment restores healing and beauty. Nature's spirits become reality and a part of daily life. Nature's spirits will be discussed in greater detail later in this writing.

In order to appreciate and establish a relationship with nature, you must spend time surrounded by it. Don't be in a hurry. Take your time. Take a walk. Involve yourself with some aspect of nature that resonates with you. Get out on the land and walk around it. Go at about half your usual pace, using this time for meditation. Be observant. Study and enjoy the trees, birds, animals, plants, weather, sky, and clouds. Notice colors, the behavior of animals and birds, as well as the number of each. Remember to pay attention or you will miss opportunities that may present themselves. Keep a journal, relax, enjoy, slow down. Use all of your senses: vision, hearing, smell . . . feel and rejoice.

Perhaps a list may help to lead you in growing your relationship with nature. Over time, it all becomes automatic. Once the connection is made, it will never disappear as long as you continue to nurture it.

1. Be involved . . . bird watching, walking, study and identify plants and trees.
2. Study . . . learn about one plant, animal, or tree a week.
3. Meditate in nature . . . send positive thoughts and prayers, use your intuition.
4. Listen . . . acknowledge a bird calling, fragrances, colors, the quiet stillness of nature.
5. Read . . . tales and myths, be guided to new wonders.
6. Honor nature . . . develop and expand your relationship by:
    - Leaving the natural world unchanged
    - Respecting the environment and all habitats
    - Planting a tree. A tree is a living creation. It eats,

breathes, and circulates life. It is a home and shelter for many creatures. It provides oxygen for the earth.
7. Be grateful . . . be a caretaker, offer prayers, and remain in balance within yourself and your surroundings.

Learning to Receive and Understand Messages from Nature

How do we interpret signs, omens, and messages? There have been many types, forms, and expressions dating back to the biblical era. There is one we can all use. It is the art of nature-speak.

We all have gifts. We do not all have the same gifts. But, we all receive messages from nature because we are a part of nature. Learning to read the signs and messages from nature is easy and rewarding. Let's examine intuition first. You must be relaxed and in a spiritual state, quiet and observant. Meditation and prayer are excellent for receiving intuitive messages. When you receive an intuitive message, it is critical to not question it. Just receive and believe. You should also be aware that Spirit will give us information in more than one form and usually more than one time. I believe we are given messages at least three times and in different forms or methods. So, when receiving intuitive messages, be conscious of what else you receive: a color, fragrance, sound, vision, etc. With practice, receiving intuitive messages will become easier and you will have no question as to what you are receiving. Other related help or assistance can come from totems, animals, and birds. Intuitive messages and divine guidance in other forms are helpful and supportive in our daily lives.

Connecting with Spirit is easier while being one with nature. Being calm, relaxed, peaceful, and open to what may present itself is the ideal mindset. Feel the power of nature. Be reverent and respectful of it. Remain positive and be patient. Remember, nature has tremendous healing powers and wants to share all of it with you.

All living things have their own spirit guides assigned to attend to them. We, as humans, have guardian angels, or spirits, to look after us. Sometimes known as sprites, elves, fairies, and devas, these guides remain with us throughout our lives and assist us with our every need. You will become more and more conscious of and connected to these spirit guides as you practice and evolve in your spiritual walk. The angelic kingdom has four main categories: those who work with humans, those who work with animals, those who work with the elements, and those who work with plant life. Nature's spirits are also divided into four categories: the spirit of earth, the spirit of fire, the spirit of water, and the spirit of air. For each of these, there is an archangel to watch over them. The earth is guarded by elves and gnomes and is ruled by the archangel, Uriel. Water is guarded by sea nymphs and water spirits. It is ruled by the archangel, Gabriel. Air is guarded by zephyrs, sylphs, and devas and ruled by the archangel, Raphael. Fire is guarded by salamanders and flamen and ruled by the archangel, Michael.

It is a relatively common experience for people to glimpse spirits when walking through the woods or gazing at a waterfall. However, most dismiss the experience as a trick, an optical illusion, or their imagination. Others see these spirits and refuse to accept what they have seen.

There are also a large number of people who see nature's spirits and welcome them. There are countless people who see nature's spirits but have not talked about them with others. It is sad to think that, in today's world, we still cannot talk about spirit guides and nature's spirits.

How do you see nature's spirits? It starts, of course, with being with nature. Approach nature with an open mind. Again, be reverent and respectful. When the time is right, the invisible helpers will make themselves known to you.

Nature's spirits are found all over the world and can be experienced in several different ways. There can be a feeling of a light brush or caress. One can "see" them with the mind's eye or by normal vision. As mentioned earlier, they can come in the form of a fragrance. Some experience a "presence." Spirits have no limitations in their mode of communication.

I have had many outstanding and awesome experiences with spirits. I see colors and orbs during my prayer sessions and sporadically throughout my day. Visions appear during meditation and healing ceremonies. There have been countless experiences with totems. My main totems are the bear and eagle. They appear frequently and help guide me daily. My spirit guides and I have a very loving and working relationship. Many are friends and family that have crossed over but some are spirits whom I have not met in this lifetime. However, one must understand that none of this would be possible without a totally loving Heavenly Father, the Creator of All.

Like many others in my life, I have read stories about fairies and elves, but I had not experienced anything or any type of encounter that I was aware of until the last few years. In my most recent walk, the majority of my spiritual activity has been out in nature, walking through the woods, surrounded by trees and the lake. Most of my ceremonies, prayers, healings, and visions have been at a ceremonial site I call the Sacred Circle. It is located deep in the woods, below the dam. I was guided to this location and organized it like the Muskogee Indians would have done— using stones in the configuration of the four cardinal directions, Grandmother Earth, and the thirteen moons. The first time I was aware of a presence was when I noticed a tree with a large, unusual opening in its lower trunk. The opening was recessed and shaped like a heart. This particular tree is about one hundred feet from the Sacred Circle and is visible from the site. In my walk each day, I passed near the tree and would stop and offer a prayer. Orbs would appear in the heart-shaped opening. These orbs were various colors but predominantly green, blue, yellow, and red. On several occasions, during prayer, orbs would float from my hands or fingertips to the opening of the tree and disappear at the base. One morning, as I approached the tree, the heart-shaped opening looked different. The hole looked like the face of Knowledge and Wisdom . . . like the face of a wise and loving old man. Then, a large, white, and very bright-blue mist, about twenty to thirty feet wide and fifteen to twenty feet tall, formed around the tree. My prayer, which I believe was given to me, was for my total commitment to being transformed into a clairvoyant healer. I prayed that I would do good and only good with these gifts that had been given me. I vowed to be an example of love and grace in order to serve God. As my prayer progressed, spirits and spirit lights, or orbs, were everywhere in shades of green, blue-green, yellow, and red. Carter Shepard, see Chapter 11, was there, and his orb appeared on a nearby tree. Later in my ceremony, I began playing my flute, concentrating on the tree with the heart-shaped opening. I gave it the name "Tree of Wisdom and Knowledge." The blue mist remained and it covered the tree. This was a most powerful ceremony. My spirit guides, teacher, prophetic guide, and family/tribe surrounded me. Spiritual light filled the area and was accompanied by new spiritual energy that I had not experienced before. I was overcome with gratitude and honor as I accepted the blessings and gifts with fearless love.

Orbs continued to appear in the opening of the tree in the days to follow. Their colors were red, green, and blue. Very small, pale-green fairies that looked like tiny butterflies fluttered around me. A turtle also sat quietly nearby. This was new to me.

As I advised earlier, it is necessary to keep an open mind when dealing with nature and its spirits. So, I acknowledged the fairies and, as a result, they began to visit more often, along with elves. While I still stood at the Tree of Wisdom and Knowledge, I asked to go forward on this new path of my walk. I was immediately filled with strong spirit energy and a vision of a red heart.

Tree of Wisdom
Cover in Spiritual Energy
Blue Mist

I began having other experiences as well. Each morning I would find tree leaves, as though they were placed, on the stone where I sat in the Sacred Circle. On the bench where I always placed my flute and drum, there were more leaves. Each day, the leaves were there and I began counting them. I wondered if there was a message in the number that appeared. Numbers can have positive and negative meanings, so I was alert and watched for any pattern that seemed to appear. Numerology is helpful in developing an expanded vocabulary for communicating with nature. The greatest emphasis is on the single digits, one through nine. The chart below is taken from *Animal Speak* by Ted Andrews. It is a useful reference guide in numerology.

Number	Positive Aspects	Negative Aspects
1	Beginnings, originality, leader	Arrogance, dominance
2	Feminine, dreams, cooperation	Sensitivity, meddling
3	Creativity, birth, mystical	Gossipy, moody
4	Foundations, patience, builder	Stubborn, rigid
5	Versatile, change, activity	Scattered, overindulgent
6	Home, service, family	Jealous, worrisome
7	Wisdom, seeker, truth	Faithless, critical
8	Power, money, infinity	Careless, greed, authoritarian
9	Healing, understanding	Gullible, hypersensitive

(All double-digit numbers can be reduced to one of these nine by adding the two digits together. For example, 23 = 2 + 3 = 5.)

Tree of Wisdom

Orbs of green, blue, red, citrine, and yellow continued to move around at the opening of the Tree of Wisdom and Knowledge. Another turtle appeared, and I was also supported by birds, hawks, ducks, and a great blue heron during the next few days.

I made a habit of propping my walking stick against a tree branch during my morning prayers and healing ceremonies. It wasn't long before the light-green fairies began to rest on the stick. At times, there were just a few. At other times, there were many. I would pick up the stick and they would exit the end of the stick and disappear. This was an amazing sight, and I welcomed their company.

Walking Stick and Flute

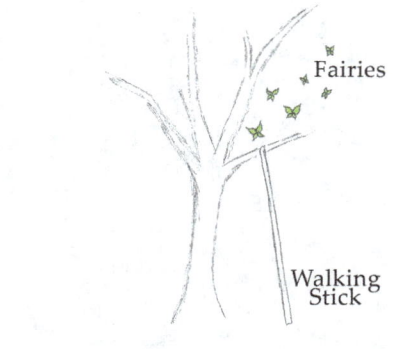

Flute

One morning, the Tree of Wisdom and Knowledge was completely covered with blue spirit light, while the heart-shaped opening was red. Fairies were playfully zipping out of the top of the walking stick and into my flute, which was hanging on a nearby branch. It reminded me of children on a playground, running around, laughing, and playing. The joyful beings seemed so carefree, and I joined in their elation. Another wonderful experience came one day when I was walking to the Sacred Circle for my morning prayers. A fairy passed close to the Tree of Wisdom. So, I stopped there, greeted all, and began playing my flute for a few moments. I then walked a short distance and sat on a wooden bench and rested. Looking back at the tree, I saw the opening was filled with green orbs.

Tree of Wisdom
Green Orbs

I got up and continued to the Sacred Circle. I greeted all spirits and said my prayers of gratefulness. As I sat on a stump inside the circle, an orb appeared in the opening of the Tree of Wisdom. The orb had the shape of a figure inside it. It looked like Aladdin's lamp. The lamp then changed to the figure of a person, facing away from me, and bending slightly. The area around it was flat and the base of the orb was green.

The figure on the green-and-tan base then lifted up two or three feet, moved off to the east, and faded away. Still sitting on the stump, a second vision appeared. With my eyes closed, I saw a gold-and-black orb moving toward me at a high-rate speed. I sat upright to welcome the spirit orb. As it came closer, it was low to the ground. It then dropped down in front of me, turned right, floated up, and faded away. I was peaceful and calm the entire time. It left me so joyful that all I could say was "Wow!"

Vision: Aladdin's Lamp

Vision
Elf—Clothed
Two Colors—Blue, Tan

There are many wonders of nature. Our own spiritual growth will allow us to see and sense that which is usually invisible to us. I have been privileged to see fairies and elves. They are part of a group called elementals. They exist without ever being reincarnated as we know it. Both of them have appeared to me in the area of the Sacred Circle. Fairies are very active and appear frequently. They are a joyous part of my ceremonies, seeming to be most active around my walking stick, flute, spiritual stone, and feather. Elves are known to be playful. They love playing tricks, which I have experienced firsthand. I found a nice feather one morning on my walk to the Sacred Circle. After completing my ceremony, I placed the feather in the flute carrying case. I walked into the house and opened the case. The feather was gone. It had only been five minutes since I put the feather in the case. I said out loud, "Where is the feather? I know you will take me to it." I retraced my steps along the lakeshore and there it was, lying out in the open path. I grinned and thanked them for returning nature's gift.

Fairies and elves bring me joy. They lift my spirits and provide guidance as well as encouragement. Their loving presence is crucial to my walk and spiritual journey. I asked Spirit if it was okay to leave them gifts from time to time and got a strong "yes." So, I began to leave pieces of candy for them. It makes me happy to give, and I believe they are very happy to receive the small tokens of love.

One very still, quiet morning, I stood looking at the heart-shaped opening in the Tree of Wisdom. There was a thin plant with three leaves growing from it. Although the air was still, the plant started swaying side to side. I picked up my flute and began playing. As I played, green light surrounded the plant and it began to move faster, in time with the music. The green light soon turned red, and I put the flute away and began the healing ceremony.

Previously, I had seen various orbs around the tree in shapes of different birds or animals. For example, I once saw a pale green, owl-shaped orb, then a citrine bear-shaped orb. All of these were unusual but did not compare to the feeling I had of a "presence."

All of nature is alive. Plants breathe, grow, adapt, and defend themselves just as we do. They stimulate the senses, heal, inspire, and are very self-sufficient. They are the basic food source for all living things. Without them, nothing else could exist. The color green has always been considered a healing color. Spending time with nature, the trees and plants in particular, allows the different shades of green to restore and revitalize us physically, mentally, and emotionally. We gain inspiration, insight, and wisdom from nature.

It has been my pleasure in the past few years to gain knowledge from all things around me. I have the God-given gift of seeing spiritual colors. These are colors that reach beyond the three-dimensional world we see with our worldly eyes. It is a very powerful dimension and one that comes from the Divine Creator.

There are nine major colors that are used in healing. They are black, blue, brown, green, orange, red, pink, white, and yellow-gold. Each color emits a different energy and is used to interpret the type of ailment that is present as well as the color to be used for healing that ailment.

To begin, black is sometimes assumed to be indicative of evil or bad omens. But this is not true. Black represents quiet strength, protection, and is associated with feminine energies such as creativity and intuition. When it appears with other colors, it can indicate a grounding. Sometimes, black is associated with mysticism, magic, and new birth.

Blue brings the energy of expression and increases perception. When encountered in nature, it always stands out. Regardless of the shade of blue, this color reflects truth and happiness. Deeper shades appear when healing is needed on both physical and spiritual levels.

Brown is one of the most common colors in nature. When plants and grasses are turning brown, we need to examine how we are using our resources. Brown is a reminder to be in balance, be practical, have our feet on the ground, and use common sense.

Green is the color of the natural world and is found throughout the plant and animal kingdom. It reflects growth, abundance, and healing. It can also be used to affirm that we are on the right path and that things are occurring in its proper time and place.

Orange expresses warmth and joy. It is often found among flowers, insects, birds, and reptiles. It reflects new energies, creativity, and new joy. When you are aware of orange, it is time to balance your emotions and recoup your energies.

Red is very often associated with love, passion, sexuality, strength, anger, and revenge. Red is a striking color in nature and captures your attention. It indicates strong energy around us and in our life. If red appears, we should use care and manage our impulsive and aggressive behavior. It could also appear if it is time to pursue new opportunities with strong energy.

Pink often contains a message regarding sensitivity or the lack thereof. It also helps soothe emotions.

White is a friend in all of nature's kingdoms. It reflects the energies of truth. White can indicate the presence of spirits around us. When white appears, be alert to a forthcoming message and follow your creative inspirations. Again, patience is essential.

Yellow-gold is a strong energy and indicates that communications are at hand. It is the time to trust your intuition and your inspirations. Do not be overly critical. A renewal of enthusiasm is coming, and a health or emotional cleansing for you or someone close to you is looming.

Nature communicates with us through our physical senses of sight, sound, smell, touch, and taste. It also uses our metaphysical sense of intuition. Think of interpreting your encounters in nature as being similar to interpreting your dreams. Signs and messages from nature are often like our dreams. If the messages are important, nature will present you with several experiences or encounters to ensure your understanding. They can be through nature or multidimensional, but the first message you receive will probably be "the one." Trust your senses. In time, your skills will sharpen and you will feel secure in your ability to comprehend what nature is trying to tell you.

Another way of receiving information and being more aware is to pay attention to directions. There are many different beliefs in different societies around the world.

The following chart shows some common guidelines when working with directions:

Direction	Traits
East	Healing, new birth, intuition
West	Emotions, renewal, visions, dreams
South	Change, trust, protection, resurrection
North	Thankfulness, knowledge, abundance

11. Carter Shepard

I never met Carter, but he is a constant in my life. Through Spirit, he has supported and encouraged me in the writing of this book.

This special chapter has to do with a wonderful learning and communication phase, spiritualism, and love. For me, this relationship started in a rather unique way. During one of my readings with Carolyn Cummings, I learned she had coauthored a book about connecting and communicating with those in the universe, or as some might say, those on the other side. After reading this book titled *What They Want You to Know*, I called Carolyn and expressed my great appreciation for this wonderful and educational book. I asked her for the phone number for the other author, Carter Shepard. I also asked if it was advisable for me to call him and thank him for his outstanding work. She said he would really enjoy hearing from me. This phone call would be my only contact with him before he crossed over. We never met in person. In 2010, I heard he was very ill. I started sending prayers for Carter. The prayers were for comfort, peace, and support. I included these prayers in my daily ceremonies. November 21, 2010, was a clear, sunny, beautiful day. Billie and I were outside doing some gardening. Midmorning, I heard and then saw a small, brown bird pecking on my bedroom window. It pecked several times then flew a short distance, landed on a tree branch, then flew away. My mother told me many years ago that birds pecking on a window is a sign that someone has crossed over. She had experienced this many times in her own spiritual work. Since I knew Carter was very ill, I immediately thought of him. There were two other birds, a great blue heron and great white egret, acting in a somewhat unusual way. They were both walking back and forth in the front yard, coming closer and closer to the house. Earlier, in my morning ceremonies, I saw a vision of an orb. This orb was in two colors. The orb had a green center which was surrounded by the color red. The orb moved from my right to my left.

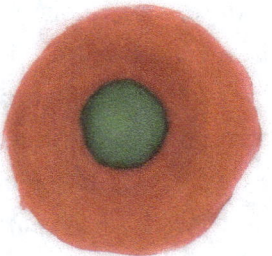

Orb—Prayer, Comfort, Peace

That evening, during meditation, I saw a bright-yellow orb. The color yellow means confidence, optimism, and enthusiasm.

The next day, November 22, I heard an owl hoot three different times. It was at 4:30 p.m., an unusual time for owls to be calling. On November 28, I learned that Carter had crossed over on November 21, 2010, the day the bird was pecking on my window.

I performed special prayers for Carter Shepard that day. In the midst of prayer, a vision of a person appeared on a tree directly in front of me and about fifteen feet away. In the vision, the color of the person was white and surrounded by a yellow glow. Outside of the yellow glow was another glow in the color green. When the vision faded away, I asked Carter, "If that is you, could I see that vision again?" Almost at once, an orb appeared in the same location. This time, there was no figure in the vision but the colors remained bright yellow and green.

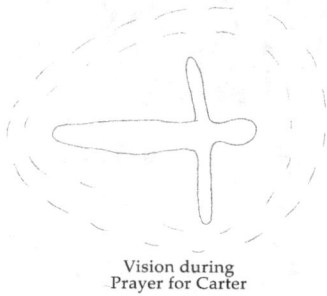

Vision during
Prayer for Carter

The following is a daily accounting of spiritual contact and communications from Carter to his family and loved ones:

November 21, 2010: Carter crossed over.

November 22, 2010: I saw a bright-yellow light late in the evening and strong animal activity.

November 28, 2010: During my morning meditation and prayers, I said a special prayer for Carter. A vision of the figure of a person in white color appeared. This was my first communication with Carter after his passing.

November 30, 2010: A hawk appeared overhead, flying east to west. Then, three turkey vultures circled directly overhead. Walking to the Sacred Circle, a lone turkey vulture circled several times. Once I reached the Sacred Circle, I said prayers for Carter's soul. The vision of a red orb appeared and remained for a substantial length of time. Purple and violet colors appeared, then a glow appeared behind the red orb. These are strong spiritual colors and I knew this message was from Carter. He wanted me to be aware of new spiritual growth in my life.

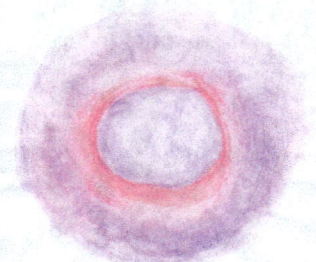

Carter's Spiritual Message
Sent in an Orb

December 2, 2010: Along with my own personal messages, Carter was sending messages through myself to his loved ones. I telephoned Carter's family to inquire if they were interested in the spiritual messages I had received. They were very anxious to hear and grateful to me for passing them along. They asked that I stay in close contact.

December 3, 2010: I had flute music playing while praying for Carter and his family.

During the morning ceremonies, I asked Carter to come in. The same multicolored orbs with a yellow center and surrounded by a green glow that changed to blue appeared on the same tree where they appeared in earlier ceremonies. I asked about the hearts, some with breaks in them, that I had seen around the property. The intuitive message: He didn't want loved ones to be brokenhearted, but to be thankful for all experiences in this life as they are part of our lessons, evolution, and teachings.

I finished my morning ceremonies and returned to the garage. As I walked in, I was immediately struck by a very profound image. To my surprise, a bald eagle, in vivid color, adorned the far wall of the room. Its head was turned to the side, displaying the penetrating eye and majestic beak. The head and neck were golden yellow and white. A drab olive green surrounded the entire image. Carter told me to expect new growth in my spirituality and I knew that the eagle was there to guide me. From that day on, the eagle became my main totem and spiritual animal.

Vision during Prayer
"Don't be broken-hearted."
—Carter to his family

Vision: Bald Eagle

I continued my daily ceremonies with prayers and healings. Carter's orbs of green and yellow were also a constant companion. The orbs always appeared in the same colors and at the same location on the same tree. I named the tree "Carter's Tree" since the appearance of his orbs had become somewhat of a ritual. I called Carter's family from time to time, giving them any message that Carter wished to convey.

December 5, 2010: I had a vision of an arrow pointing upward with an intuitive message of "Doing the right things." This was followed by the figure of a red heart, which was common in the messages from Carter. Three orbs then appeared. The first orb was green, the next orb was gold, and the next orb was bright green.

December 6, 2010: I saw orbs with a figure of a violet heart displayed on Carter's Tree. The color violet then appeared in the palm of my right hand. Intuitively, I knew Carter wanted to convey love and healing to his family. When I called them later to pass this message along, they told me they had seen yellow and green orbs on their bedroom wall that morning. They questioned whether or not this was Carter and I affirmed that it, indeed, was him. Carter sent them to the family for emotional healing. They asked how they could get closer to Carter. I told them to meditate.

December 8, 2010: I saw the vision of an orb shaped like a pyramid. The top was green and the bottom was yellow. Inside the triangle, there was a very bright-blue heart. Carter was sending love, peace, and comfort to his family, by way of the heart and the color blue.

One Man's Spiritual Journey to Healing with Color Energy

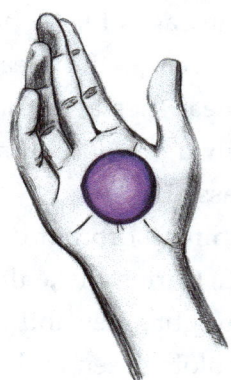

Carter's Tree

Vision—Orb from Carter
To family—Love, Peace, Comfort

December 11, 2010: While praying for Carter's loved ones, I saw a very large, red orb in front of me. I asked, "If this is for Carter's loved ones, show the color red in my left hand." Boom! A large, red orb immediately appeared in the palm of my left hand. Then, I saw a large, red path of light in the woods. Very strong colors appeared on top of the house and these colors were moving! This was so powerful that I thought to myself, *Wow!*

In daily ceremonies, I continued to see red orbs from Carter. I confirmed each time that they were messages for his family. Animal spirit guides were also around such as the great blue heron and wood duck. I also began to hear messages that told me to live fearlessly. Carter was definitely a presence in my life and our relationship grew as the days passed.

December 13, 2010: I saw a light within an orb but couldn't tell what it was, so I asked, "If that is you, Carter, make the light brighter." At once, the orb color became bright green and yellow, followed by red, violet, and blue. The colors green and yellow are for emotional healing, red is for strength, violet is a spiritual color, and blue is for love and support. I gave this message to family members and, as always, they were grateful. After our phone conversation, I asked Spirit to send these colors to Carter's loved ones. I closed my eyes and saw a small, green orb, then I heard a woodpecker on a nearby tree. This was my teacher letting me know the message had been sent.

December 22, 2010: During my morning meditation and prayers, I saw a figure of a person in the woods, just south of the house. The figure was green and yellow, Carter's colors. It lingered a few minutes and disappeared.

Shape of a Man

In the afternoon ceremony, a large, red orb appeared in the sky, directly overhead. Inside the orb, a turkey vulture flew, moving with the orb. The vulture remained inside the red orb, never leaving its parameters. It soon disappeared in a southerly direction. Very shortly, another turkey vulture flew just above the trees, and circled directly over my head. It too, was inside a red orb. This happens frequently.

December 23 and 24, 2010: During my ceremonies at the Sacred Circle, Carter appeared as flashing colors of blue and green on Carter's Tree. He manifested red and yellow orbs as well. He was again sending his undying love and healing to his family.

December 28, 2012: I asked Spirit if I should do a distant healing for Carter's loved ones and received a definite "yes." As soon as the ceremony began, vivid colors of yellow, green, blue, red, and violet emerged on his tree. A red heart, which I had come to know as Carter's signature, and two heart-shaped orbs also appeared. They were citrine with a red glow.

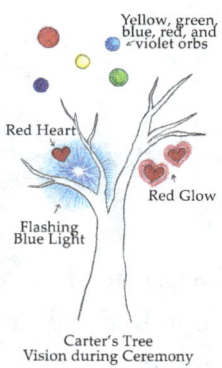

Carter's Tree
Vision during Ceremony

December 29, 2012: I saw a large, yellow orb with three hearts inside the orb. The three hearts inside the orb were a brighter yellow than the orb itself.

Lee Hillberg

December 31, 2010: Green and yellow orbs were prominent in the morning ceremony at the Sacred Circle. When I was done, I returned to the garage. A new development in my spiritual growth was the projection of brightly colored orbs from my fingertips. Sometimes, orbs would shoot from my spiritual stone as well. So, I occasionally played with this new spiritual "tool." I set my drum and flute on the workbench, extended my arm, and pointed my finger at the far wall. Bright-green, yellow, red, and blue orbs shot from my finger and across the garage. They slid across the wall, floated to another wall, and stopped. After a moment, they faded away. I pointed my finger again and the same thing happened. I repeated several times, each time in awe of my spiritual light show. The colors were strong and the orbs moved in straight, smooth paths.

Spiritual Message from Carter

I walked outside the garage and saw a very bright, blue-green orb approximately one hundred feet away and about ten feet off the ground. There were several red orbs in the sky. A turkey vulture was flying inside one of the orbs and they moved together. There were four other turkey vultures flying in the same vicinity. I started walking toward the house. As I walked, I glanced down at my hands. My eyes widened and my jaw dropped when I saw that they were totally covered in colors. As I watched, the colors began to change slowly. They went from orange, to indigo, to purple, to green, then yellow and violet. They were intense and lasting for quite a long period of time. I received an intuitive message at the same time saying, "Stronger spiritual healing has started." This was powerful and I felt a surge of spiritual energy throughout my body.

January 3, 2011: I looked for Carter's colors on his tree at the Sacred Circle. They were there, but the colors were very weak. I asked to see them again and they came forward with a burst of green. It was an intuitive message that something was changing. It was at this time the family ceased to communicate with me and there were no further messages from Carter to his family.

Carter continues to be a major part of my spiritual guidance today and is at all ceremonies. His colors, green and yellow, consistently show up on Carter's Tree. His spiritual presence and support will continue in my journey. I am surely blessed.

A special comment: The first thing that happens when you cross over into the spiritual realm is an accounting of your life, which is also called a review. The review is what your soul has learned in this lifetime, here in the physical world. Think of it as going through immigration or various other checkpoints. There are several goals in each lifetime. Review is the summary of the life and an assessment of whether or not you achieved your goals. The length of time spent in review varies based on the soul's experiences in that lifetime. When the soul is in review, it is not available for any other activities or contact with the physical world. It seems wise to review your life before crossing over. What does this mean? Look at your life in a truthful way, with clear eyes, and change what you can before you cross over. Make amends for any transgression and better your position for a faster review.

Endeavor to be open minded, strive wholeheartedly and with great purpose to overcome fears. Replace fear with love. Know that there is a home waiting for you that will embrace you regardless of your choices. Come to balance with your karma and love others as well as yourself. Appreciate the fact that you are special. You are a soul capable of deep, unconditional love. If you do not love yourself, you cannot give love, nor can you receive it.

In Carter's crossing, his soul was almost immediately available. This speaks to his life here on earth and his evolution into the spirit world. Carter was a Christian. He was a teacher to many seeking spiritual growth. He was also a student and practitioner of metaphysics and spirituality for almost thirty years. He is one of my spiritual guides and I continue to learn from him.

12. Healings

All healings come from God. God gives the colors to apply and the timeframe for healing. I am only an instrument for his purposes.

In prayer, we talk to God. In meditation, God talks to us. Not necessarily in words. He talks through nature, through others, and through intuition, just to name a few. I have learned to listen and watch for communication from God. I believe God answers all prayers. No thought, word, or deed goes unnoticed by our Creator.

During meditation, I have experienced many visions. They are always very clear and, in fact, in color. I trust in my intuition and follow the directions given. Once you become observant, you realize that all of nature is communicating with us. You learn to see with your eyes open and with your eyes closed. And you learn to use these messages in healing. Anyone can heal. We can all learn to apply energies that aid and facilitate the healing process. This applies to the physical, emotional, mental, and spiritual aspects of our lives.

My daily prayer and healing ceremonies are held at the Sacred Circle, deep in the woods, or other designated spots at my home. The house sits on approximately thirty-eight acres with a lake and surrounded by woods. Earlier, I described the arrangement of stones and totems at the Sacred Circle. It is a design used by the Muskogee/Creek with an outer circle of thirteen stones, representing the moon cycle of a year. The center of the circle has four stones which are set in the cardinal directions of north, south, east, and west. In the center of the four stones is a larger stone, or boulder. It represents Grandmother Earth. The area above the circle represents our Creator. I sometimes use another area that is closer to the house, near the garage. It is arranged in the same fashion. I call it the Ceremony Circle. A large bear totem stands near the edge of both Circles, while a small bear totem rests on the center stones. The eagle totem takes a prominent position as well. There is a totem of a horse, named Bronco, rearing up on its hind legs, positioned at the perimeter of the Ceremony Circle. It is reminiscent of my younger days in the Black Hills. Memories of rodeos and cowboys parading through the streets during the Days of '76 celebration flood my mind when I look at this totem. The horse totem is a favorite spot of some of the spirits who visit me. I often see colored orbs resting on it during my daily ceremonies. The Prayer Temple is the gazebo located in the woods on the southeast side of the house. This location is good for rainy days. Most of my daily ceremonies are held at the Sacred Circle or the Ceremony Circle. I am drawn to these sites and feel a strong spiritual connection to them.

Ceremonial Circle

When I first began healing prayers, I started seeing bright colors while feeling powerful spiritual energy. Many times, my spirit stone took on the same colors I was seeing. The same thing would happen with the marker stones in the Sacred Circle. All stones would be the same color. Sometimes, the stones changed color, but still one color for all of them. Then, I noticed that the same color would appear on the palm of my hand. If I pointed at an object, the color would appear on that object. The colors usually faded away after a while, although there were times when they remained on my hands when I returned to the house.

It is important to reiterate that the appropriate colors to be used in healings are provided by Spirit. There have been times when I have seen a color and began focusing on it only to have it change to another color. This happens from time to time. When it does, I simply change my focus to the new color. I concentrate on the color and apply its energy as long as the color shows. Once it fades, it is time to stop.

We have studied and reviewed healing with color, how to apply color for healing, and other influencing factors such as nature, animals, and spirits. The amount of healing energy available to us is as unlimited as the universe. I mentioned earlier that color therapy is a way of being proactive to improve our holistic health. We are employing preventative care to maintain our health or the health of those who request it. We learn to take responsibility for our own well-being and to connect to the natural elements as well as our Creator, God. This type of healing, or holistic healing, is meant to find the source of the problem rather than only treating the symptoms. The cause and cure lie within us. The human body has wondrous restoring powers. The divine love of God sparks a desire for health and balance. Being healed is to be made whole, or one with God, the Universe, our neighbors, and ourselves. Many refer to healings as miracles when, in fact, miracles are not unusual at all. Miracles are supposed to happen and do happen.

Traditional medicine and doctors serve a critical role in our health, but we should not overlook proven alternative, spiritual methods. These methods work in harmony with traditional medicine. Remember, God is the greatest healing source and He is always available and willing to address our every need.

Color therapy is not a cure for every health issue. You cannot use color to replace a medical prescription. Only healthcare professionals are qualified in the diagnosis and treatment of medical conditions. However, it is a method of working in total cooperation with professional medicine. Many times, I have been involved with those who were undergoing treatment of cancer. Some were taking chemotherapy while others were not. There were those who elected to bypass professional medicine and use color therapy alone. In all cases, we were working in harmony with Spirit for the benefit of the individual being treated.

You may ask yourself if everyone who asks for healing will actually be totally healed. The answer is no. It is up to God whether or not someone will be rid of an affliction while on this earth. Sometimes, He has other plans. There have been times when Spirit told me not to perform healings on certain individuals. Other times, I was told to stop after just a few applications. God gives the colors to apply as well as the approval or timeframe for the healing.

This writing is used to describe some of the instances where color energy was effective when used by me or others in the past. The majority of healings I have conducted have been from a distance. In other words, the person needing healing was not with me. I have found that distance healings and in-person healings are equally effective. God is the source of all healing so time and distance are of no concern. Of course, in-person healings allow for direct communication between me and the individual. I can explain the process of both in-person and distance healing as we go.

Now, let's look at some of my experiences with people who have asked for intervention and their results. I will start by describing the first healing I was asked to perform. Billie was suffering from arthritis in her lower back, right leg, knee, and ankle. I began by reading her aura. It is not necessary to read everyone's aura, but it can be beneficial in assessing their condition. Immediately, brilliant gold and green lights began to flash around her body. They were like lightning bolts, strong, intense, and dazzling. I was overwhelmed with electrical energy and vibrations to the point that I became weak. It was one of the strongest and most powerful auras I had ever seen. As I gazed at the amazing energy field surrounding Billie, my eyes fluttered and I felt a torrent of energy surge across my head, neck, and shoulders. It was difficult to focus as my vision became blurred by the radiating energy. Finally, I was able to see the colors appearing in the afflicted areas.

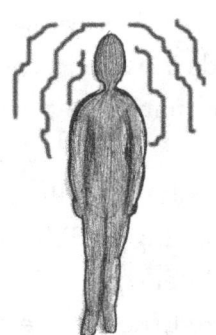
Figure of a Man Shown as a Dark Inset

Figure of a Woman—Color, Violet

I asked her to sit in a chair and I explained what I was going to do. First, I prayed and asked God for her healing. Then, using my hands as I do in all in-person healings, I balanced the chakras by visualizing and applying white crystalline color from her crown chakra to her base chakra. As I was doing this, Billie said she felt a powerful pressure being drawn from her head. Without touching her, I passed my hands three to six inches over the afflicted areas of the lower back, legs, knees, and feet. Violet and blue appeared in these areas. However, Billie was seeing the color yellow. As I moved to her base chakra, I concentrated on the color red even though it did not become visible to me. I did see yellow in the abdomen area, telling me that she had some digestive issues that needed to be addressed. As I continued, the colors that had appeared on her would then appear in my palm. By passing my hands over her, I transferred the energy of the colors to her body. She said she felt a tremendous sensation of heat. She also described a "pulling" sensation when I passed my hands over her liver. Soon, the colors began to fade and I knew that the treatment was complete. I finished by balancing the chakras again and saying a prayer of thanksgiving for her healing.

A few days later, I was at the Sacred Circle alone, preparing to do a healing on Billie. She was experiencing pain in her back, right leg, foot, and ankle, and her hands. As I prayed, colors appeared on the marker stones. Then, a dark vision of a man appeared, followed by the vision of a woman. The woman's right side was entirely violet.

I remembered that I had seen the same color on Billie's right side earlier. I continued with prayers for healing of Billie's pain then followed with balancing her chakras. After concluding with a prayer of thanksgiving for the healing, I returned to the house to get Billie. I called for her to come outside. When she came to the door, her brow was indigo and her cheeks were glowing red. Wow! I was excited that Spirit had heard my prayers and already began the healing process. What a start for the healing ceremony!

Once we reached the Sacred Circle, the colors started appearing. They covered her skin and clothing as well as my hand. As I passed my hand about three inches over her, the colors shot ahead to her body.

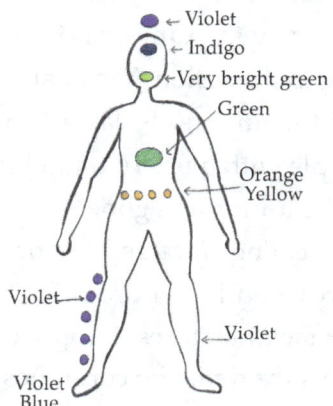
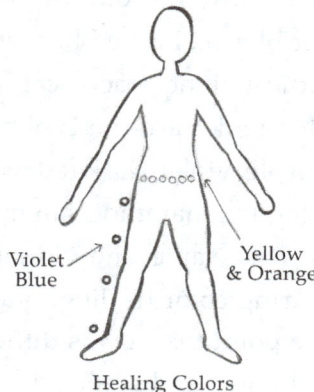

Healing Colors

Violet and blue covered her right side. Her brow was swathed in violet while her abdomen was green, orange, and yellow.

This healing was much like those discussed earlier. Spirit provided the same conditions and colors that had been seen before.

Over the next few weeks, I continued the healing ceremonies for Billie. Each time, colors would vary slightly but blue and violet would always appear. Colors other than what I focused on would sometimes emerge. I learned not to question this. I said before, and will reiterate, that God is the source of all healing. His Spirit directs the healing and the colors are always given by Him. Do not worry about it. Simply trust and use your intuition.

What were the results of these healings? Billie experienced less pain, greater flexibility, and some reduction in swelling. The arthritis did not disappear but was substantially reduced, leaving her with a greater quality of life.

I performed in-person healings on another woman in her midfifties. Her doctor discovered a growth in her right breast.

It was suspicious and the doctor wanted to do a mammogram to rule out cancer. Her totem was the turtle. During the healing ceremony, the outline of a violet-colored tumor appeared on her blouse. I asked her where the doctor saw the tumor and she indicated the exact location I was seeing in the vision. Violet and blue-violet are the typical colors used for tumors. I was given purple, violet, dark red, white, then purple with blue. Two weeks later, the mammogram indicated that the tumor was gone.

This same individual asked for healing for depression. During color healing, blue and green covered her entire face to the point that it was difficult to see her facial features. I applied light blue and green and the depression subsided. She continues to experience occasional depression but is relieved by the same color therapy.

There is a woman in Georgia for whom I have performed both in-person and distance healings. She is in her midsixties and suffers from a noncancerous tumor in her right ear. It is an acoustic neuroma. I have had the same condition and will discuss it later in this chapter. She was treated at Emory Medical Clinic. I asked Spirit if I should do a healing for her and received a bright-green color surrounded by a red trim in the palm of my right hand. In my experience, this meant I should proceed with the healing ceremony. Spirit provided white, red, purple, blue, orange, citrine, sage green, pink, violet, and indigo. She called a few weeks later to inform me that an MRI revealed there had been a 20 percent reduction in the size of the tumor.

Later, I performed healings on the same woman for ongoing blood-pressure, emotional, and intestinal issues. Blue, green, orange, red, yellow, and white were provided for emotional and blood-pressure healing while yellow and green attended to the intestinal problems. After reading her aura one day, I noticed an increase in the color yellow. I called her to ask what was happening with her and she said she had been dealing with serious relationship issues. That explained the intense-yellow color appearing in her aura.

Long-distance healing, sometimes known as absentee healing, is very effective. It may be difficult for us to comprehend as our minds are limited, but it transcends reality. Energy operates on all levels and in all dimensions.

There are several guidelines I use when conducting distance healings. It involves concentration, timing, and transmission of healing energy. Remember that you must control your thoughts in order to transmit color energy to another. By concentrating on the individual, healing energy can be sent regardless of time and space. Start by acquiring a witness. A witness is something tangible such as a photo, address, or other identifying item of your subject that you have with you during the session. It is important to focus on the individual as if he or she is actually there with you. As you do in an in-person healing, start by balancing the chakras. Focus on the area in need of balance. Many times during distance healing, the colors will move in the direction of the person being healed. In other words, they seem to fly away.

My first distance healing involved a person with a nervous disorder. As a witness, I was provided with his name, age, photo, and a description of the disorder. After balancing the chakras, I passed my hand over his photo and was shocked by what I saw. The color purple was so strong that I could no longer see his face. Spirit was telling me that this individual was in need of help and would benefit from color therapy.

I conducted two healing sessions a week for this person. As healing progressed, Spirit provided me with the color purple, indigo, violet, blue, yellow, and white. At times, pink, orange, and light green were also applied. He also attended sessions with a medical professional during this time. The disorder cleared after several months and the condition remains in remission.

Distance healings were conducted for a variety of people of different ages and conditions. Requests for healing came from a wide range of channels, including family, referrals, and chance meetings. I use the word "chance" but, in actuality, I know that these meetings were Spirit directed. As life dictates, the afflictions included colds, pain, anxieties, arthritis, high blood pressure, cancer, Parkinson's disease, and heart problems, just to name a few.

In February and March of 2011, I performed distance healings on a woman, a neighbor of ours, with cancer, diabetes, and heart problems. She had been receiving treatment by medical professionals and had spent some time in the hospital. During healing prayers for her, I enlisted the help of her totem, a hummingbird, and applied white, black, purple, indigo, dark blue/aqua, and orange colors. After performing ceremonies for several weeks, I received a message from Spirit: "You have done enough." I stopped color treatment and started prayers of comfort on a weekly basis. She crossed over on February 19, 2014. During my prayer ceremony on February 21, 2014, the colors pink and orange appeared twice in my right hand. Then, on the twenty-second, I received a vision of a three-pronged image. It was a salmon color and fringed by light green. I didn't know the significance of this vision at that time.

We attended the funeral services for this woman. As we walked in the chapel, I was immediately struck by the arrangement of flowers behind the casket. At the top of the tier of arrangements sent by friends and family was the arrangement Billie and I sent. It was gladiolas with light-green leaves in the exact form and color I had seen in my hand two days prior. This was our deceased friend's way of sending us thanks for the healing prayers that had been sent her way.

In February 2013, I performed distance healing for a young man in his late twenties. He had a cancerous mass in the upper lobe of his left lung and was being treated by doctors at Emory Hospital. I enlisted his totem, a beaver, and applied the colors violet, red, blue, yellow, white, and pink. In the healing visions, I saw these colors in the form of what appeared to be organs of the body. My fingers turned orange. Orange is the color of the second chakra and represents joy and wisdom. Intuitively, I knew this was a sign that he was on his way to being cured. Soon, surgeons removed the mass and he has remained cancer-free.

In 2011, another male subject, a sixty-five-year-old man living in Arizona, had glaucoma. The pressure in both eyes had reached a critical level, over twenty. The normal level of pressure in the eye ranges from twelve to twenty-two millimeters of mercury. He was being treated by a doctor but seeing no improvement. I began performing healing prayers for him twice a week using his totem, the bear, and colors indigo and royal blue. These are the most beneficial colors for glaucoma. I was also given white, green, red, dark red, blue, yellow, and orange to use during my ceremonies for him. Two months into color treatment, I suggested that he switch to another doctor, which he did. When the new doctor checked the pressure in his eyes, the instrument recorded a pressure of twelve. The doctor retested, then checked his equipment for the possibility of equipment failure. There was no equipment failure. Twelve was an accurate reading, and the doctor was amazed. He was retested in 2015. The pressure had climbed back over twenty millimeters of mercury. I returned to distance healing and soon, without medical intervention, the pressure dropped to ten in the left eye and eleven in the right. The doctors were once again astounded. Miracle? Of course. But remember, miracles are supposed to happen!

In November 2011, I was asked to perform color healing on a fifteen-year-old girl with brain cancer. She was being treated by a doctor and receiving chemotherapy. I enlisted a dove as her totem and applied white, violet, red, yellow, blue, purple, and indigo. I began with two healings a week in November and concluded in May 2012 when she was declared cured and released by her medical professionals.

A further note on this color healing ending in May 2012: I was not aware of any details concerning the start or finishing date of any chemotherapy treatments she received. I started and finished color therapy based on guidance from Spirit. The chemotherapy and color healing ended at the same time.

Today, this young lady is cancer-free, is entering her third year of college, and is considering a career in the medical field. Her name is Harleigh Sohler and she resides in Georgia.

A thirty-nine-year-old man in Georgia had colon cancer in 2011. He was scheduled for surgery in October of that year but canceled it. He decided he did not want to undergo the surgery or receive chemotherapy. I began color healing on September 22, 2011, and continued through May 26, 2012. Using a cougar as his totem, I applied blue and blue-green followed by pink and purple every six days because these are the most beneficial colors for this ailment. White, blue, citrine, violet, red, orange, indigo, yellow, purple, pink, and aqua were also used. The colors would appear in my hand then "fly" off or away from my fingers, disappearing into the distance. At the conclusion of color treatment, this individual was declared cancer free by his doctors.

During the past few years, my hearing has become a problem. Hearing tests at Auburn University Medical Center showed significant loss in both ears. Further tests revealed the need for hearing aids. While the aids improved my ability to hear, my

One Man's Spiritual Journey to Healing with Color Energy

hearing was actually declining. In 2010, my right ear showed a sharp decrease. The doctors recommended that I see a specialist to determine the cause of the dramatic decline in hearing. Since there was no pain associated with the hearing loss, the doctor ordered an MRI. It revealed a tumor in my right ear that spread across the nerves in the hearing canal. He recommended that I see yet another specialist for treatment of the tumor. In the meantime, I performed healing ceremonies for the condition and was told by Spirit to apply color as it was the appropriate treatment. However, Spirit also said to follow the medical advice of my physicians. The new specialist was at Emory University in Atlanta. He diagnosed it as an acoustic neuroma. It was a noncancerous, slow-growing tumor, but should be watched. I was told to return for a retest in six months.

I began color treatments and healing ceremonies two to three times a week. Intuitively, Spirit advised me to use purple, which shrinks tumors, and yellow on my right ear. I also applied blue, indigo, red, green, brown, and white. Later, during a reading with Carolyn Cummings, Spirit sent Mother in to confirm that these were the proper colors to be used and that the tumor would dissolve over time.

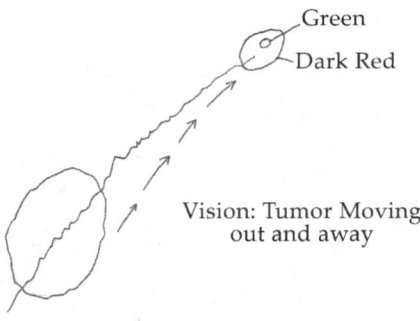

In May 2012, I was getting weak colors on the tumor and received a vision. The vision showed the tumor moving out and away. My feeling was that the tumor was gone. However, further MRIs showed an image that remains the same size as the original image in 2010. There has been no change in the size of the tumor since then nor have there been any more conditions related to an active tumor in the past six years. Is this a cure? Spirit confirms that it is gone, and I accept the healing and give thanks.

13. Lessons from Spirit

We are surrounded by spiritual beings whose primary purpose is to provide guidance in our spiritual growth and help us achieve our life's goals.

Why are we here? Most of us have asked this question from time to time. We come to the physical world, Earth, to learn lessons. Lessons that are ours alone. The primary purpose of every lifetime comes from our personal choices and decisions to learn to love. We chose to return to Earth, lifetime after lifetime, in order to master the ability to love. We yearn to love ourselves and love others as God intended. We also want to learn to live without fear in a world that presents us with endless opportunities and challenges.

The good news is that we have an unlimited army of help, spiritual beings who are working constantly in our best interest. Your teacher and protectors are waiting patiently to be welcomed and invited into your life.

There are many spirits, angels, archangels, and guardian angels who God has provided for our guidance and help. There is, in fact, a limitless number of guides. Many times, God communicates with us through His intermediaries. When we communicate with spirit guides and angels, we are sending messages directly to God. Fortunately, by contacting our guides and angels, we are much closer to the creative intelligence behind the universe.

There are different names given for those that are here for us. I will simply state how I identify some of these beings. We all have a teacher who is a highly evolved spirit. Teachers are with us from birth and remain until death. Guardian angels are also given to us at birth and stay with us throughout our lives. Spirit guides are people who have crossed over into the next life. They are usually highly evolved souls. Many times, but not always, they are family members such as a deceased parent, sibling, or other close relative. They are primarily concerned with our spiritual growth and are prepared to help us in any way they can. They are nonjudgmental and totally understanding of our need to be independent and stand on our own. They will not offer advice unless you ask them for it. Communicate with your guides as often as you wish but ask for help only when it is really necessary. Perhaps try to talk to them once or even twice a day.

My own spiritual journey reached a new height in 2008 when, during meditation, I saw a young Indian brave kneeling on the ground. This vision was very clear. I later found out the Indian brave was me in an earlier life. I was a Muskogee/Creek Indian. At that time, I started a new study of Native Americans and spiritual growth. Also, I began to meditate on a regular basis and was blessed with many visions. Several visions were of other past lives that I had lived. I saw myself as Buddhist monk wearing a white robe with a black cord around the waist. I was young and slim, standing at the base of a mountain in front of a cave. Many of the other visions were of people who were coming back into my life. For example, Bear Heart, my teacher, Ax, and an Indian woman have all appeared to me in visions. I have also seen items such as a tomahawk and various other Indian items.

During spiritual readings with Carolyn Cummings, I received clear and positive input for my spiritual growth. I eagerly choose the spiritual path and to embark on a life of inner growth and learning. I strive to develop physical, mental, emotional, and spiritual integrity.

It is helpful to develop your own method of communication with the Creator and Spirit. Be aware of your feelings, hearing, and what you see around you at all times. Use all available resources from Spirit such as angels, nature, totems, family, and friends. They all want to help you for your good and only good.

I encourage you to meditate. If you are new to meditation, be patient, focused, and relaxed. It sometimes takes a while to connect. However, it will be well worth your effort. Once you connect and visions begin, spiritual growth is imminent. In my experience, visions have been very clear and most helpful in guidance and learning. Sometimes, the meaning of a vision will not be immediately clear but will become so in time.

I have always had a somewhat heightened sense of spiritual awareness. This was probably due to my upbringing with Mother. However, it wasn't until the last few years that I experienced daily contact with Spirit and began seeing colors and orbs.

Sometimes life's lessons can be very difficult. I firmly believe that the most difficult experiences are also our greatest learning experiences. The year 2008 was a pivotal time for me. I was assembling and restoring what was left of my life after a tumultuous divorce. The pain of that event cut deep but I leaned on the inner strength that had sustained me throughout my years. Now, I found myself facing more changes with new decisions to make. I was entering into a new relationship, one that seemed natural and blessed. I also had a growing interest in spiritualism and an awakening to my connection with Native Americans. This was all quite exciting and I eagerly accepted these changes and began a new walk that brought me closer to God and nature.

In spiritual readings with Carolyn Cummings, I connected with deceased family members, my teacher, and my spirit guides. I began my daily prayer ceremonies and became more aware of the many helpers God sent my way. I had always had a keen love of trees, birds, and animals. They took on new meaning as I now understood their contributions and guidance in my life. The relationships of totems with people became apparent, and it wasn't long before I began receiving visions and seeing spiritual colors. It was only natural that I immediately felt a part of nature.

My teacher, Ax, advised me to begin keeping a journal of my daily prayer sessions. I recorded everything from the weather of the day to the visions and colors I saw while in the midst of my ceremonies. The sounds of animals and birds were a part of the details included in the journal. Soon, I recognized the innate behavior of the red-tailed hawk, woodpecker, and other birds or animals. I took note when they responded or acted in an unusual fashion. It was Spirit's way of communicating with me.

In 2009, I met with Carolyn Cummings for another spiritual reading. Almost immediately, my brother, Bob, who had crossed over several years earlier, came in and made his presence known. Bob's life in this physical world was difficult. He was a gentle soul with a quiet demeanor. He avoided conflict but would sometimes become the victim of bullies due to his timid disposition. He and I were opposite personality types, and his life took a totally different direction to mine. He became a farmer, and I went to the air force. Although he was older than me, I always felt the need to watch after him and protect him.

At the time of this reading, it was my understanding that Bob was still going through a period of healing. He asked for my help in the process, and I was happy to oblige. He requested that I go to the Spiritual Village and gather a cup of cold, running water from the stream. I was to offer the cup of water with both hands as a bond of brotherhood and forgiveness for any transgressions that may have occurred during his life on Earth. He said this would be of great help to him and he would accept the offer as a gift from me. He thanked me in advance. The next day, I did as my brother asked and gathered a cup of water from the stream in an old piece of farm equipment that could be used as a cup. I knew Bob would approve of my choice of "chalice" because he loved farming. I smiled to myself as I took the cup and walked to the spiritual village. It felt good to reconnect with my brother.

As I walked, a crow began calling out, loud and repetitively. It was in a tree over my head. The crow then flew to the west. I knew that Bob had sent the crow and it was acknowledging his attendance in the ceremony, as well as his gratefulness for my help in his healing.

After gathering the water from the stream, I went to the center of the ceremonial area and offered a prayer. Holding the cup up with both hands, I prayed for forgiveness of any hurt feelings or anger that may have lingered between Bob or myself. I then placed the cup on the center stone. The energy level was extremely high and strong. I concluded with a prayer of thanksgiving and compassion.

Later that evening, I was sitting in a chair in the family room, quietly offering a prayer of thanks to the universe and all who attended that morning's ceremonies. Again, there was high energy all around me. Suddenly, that energy pushed me back into the chair with such force that my head was flung backward. Immediately, I instinctively knew that Bob was the source of the nudge and it was meant as a display of affection. As brothers often do, Bob was giving me a playful shove to express his love and gratitude.

In reference to the same spiritual reading with Carolyn, my teacher, Ax, also came in. He said he was giving me the gift of an arrowhead and I was to look for it at home, on our property. So, as soon as I got home, I began looking for the gift. I didn't find it. A few days later, I decided to go to the ceremonial area for a short prayer. It was getting dark and there was a light rain.

I looked around for a few minutes but determined that I wouldn't find the arrowhead due to the dim light and wet ground. Just as I was about to give up the search, a woodpecker (remember that Ax sends messages to me through the woodpecker) began pecking on a tree in front of me. I just knew that my arrowhead would be lying at the base of the tree and in plain sight. To my dismay, it was not there. I was disappointed. Suddenly, I had a strong feeling that I should look around an old fence post a short distance away. Wow! There it was! I dropped to my knees and cried tears of joy and thanksgiving for the special gift Ax had given me.

I was receiving guidance from the birds, woodpecker, red-tailed hawk, and crows on a daily basis. Purple, white, gold, and red colors were appearing around me regularly as well. Colored orbs began to appear in my room at night. The vision of a black bear appeared often during my prayers.

Early one morning, I was working in the garden when I heard a red-tailed hawk calling. There was something unusual, or special, about this particular call. So, I walked to the ceremonial area and prayed. As I talked to Spirit, I received a very powerful vision of a large tree. I could only see the trunk and lowest branches of the tree. A small owl was perched on the lowest branch, while other birds were flying around the branches just above the owl. I am not sure what type of birds they were, but they appeared to be doves. As the birds landed on the branches, a very bright, white light appeared and the birds changed into stars. At the same time, the excited calls of crows filled the air. The vision subsided and I walked back to the garden. Two geese flew overhead and landed on the lake in front of me. This was a very powerful vision, so I called Carolyn to help me clarify the meaning. She said that I had been visited by angels and they were delivering the message, "enlightenment."

One Man's Spiritual Journey to Healing with Color Energy

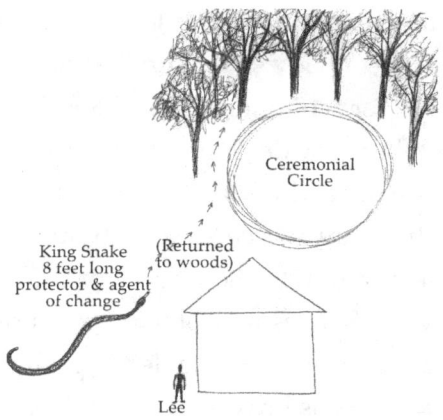

I began reading about the red-tailed hawk, owl, crow, and goose since they were the birds delivering the messages. I also received more visions. The face of a young Indian man appeared one day. I soon learned that he was my teacher, Ax. Another vision included a middle-aged Indian woman standing in front of a Muskogee tupa. Orbs continued to hover around me during meditation and prayers. Figures were sometimes visible in the center of the orbs. Snakes were also visiting quite frequently.

In April 2009, purple orbs would appear at various times during the night. Mother's orb is always with me during my evening prayers. She often rests on an Indian doll that sits on my shelf. One night, I awoke to see her orb in the shape of a heart. She was sending her love, as usual.

During meditation at that time, I received many visions. Some included the face of an Indian man, the eyes of a black bear, a man's eyes and mouth, a fox, and a wolf. They appeared as a sign of healing, insight, new teaching, and new knowledge that was coming my way. Later, I learned that the Indian face was that of Bear Heart, and the eyes and mouth belonged to Billie's father.

Multicolored orbs appeared daily and moved in different directions. I found a lot of feathers along my path. Snakes of all kinds made themselves at home around the house and on the lake. At times, there were so many snakes on the lake that it looked like a race track. There were cottonmouths, water snakes, king snakes, and many others. The snake denotes rebirth, resurrection, initiation, and wisdom. It is a symbol of death, or death of an old way and birth of a new. The shamans see snake activity as an underworld initiation or the crossing into the underworld for transformation in the state of being. Snakes and other reptiles often make their homes near water or swamps where decomposition occurs. These places are where the old is broken down and the new is built up. The shamans refer to these areas as doorways to the underworld. The cottonmouth snake is native to swamps and marshes. As with other venomous creatures, they are associated with healing and detoxification of life. They often signal that the chemistry of life is about to change. When they show up, you can expect death and rebirth to occur in some area of your life. Look for a change in conditions that will lead to new life.

Vision: "A visit by Angels"

In mid-May 2010, about four o'clock in the afternoon, I was walking to the garage with my flute for my afternoon ceremony. I put one foot on the step and looked to my left. About twelve feet away, there was the largest snake I have ever seen! It wasn't moving

... just lying totally still and looking directly at me. It was black and approximately eight feet long and four inches wide. I knew it was a king snake ... a protector. I stood very still and looked at the snake. This went on for a couple of minutes. I then said, "Okay, it's time to return to the woods." I knew Ax sent the snake because he wanted me to continue with the progress of rebirth. After several minutes, the snake slowly turned and very slowly slithered into the woods.

This same snake showed up again later. Since it is so big, it is easy to identify. I had been doing a healing and counseling ceremony with a client at the Sacred Circle. During the healing, we discussed snakes and their role in transformation. The message for the client was, "Let go of the old and allow the birth of the new." We also discussed his totem, the hawk, and how it is symbolic of new messages.

As the client was driving away, he saw this same large snake lying across the driveway. He had to wait for it to move out of the way before he could proceed. In another hundred yards, there was a red-tailed hawk perched on a nearby tree. He immediately called me on his cell phone to say, "Wow! I can't believe this!" He won't forget the message he received that day.

Initiations are new beginnings or rebirth. The initiation into the underworld deals with dangerous interactions. However, they are intended to only destroy the inflated personality, the fear-riddled mask that tyrannizes our individuality. One doesn't gain understanding of initiation by reading books, though intellectual clues and stimuli can be helpful. It comes through total change in the direction of one's life. The cottonmouth snake is a guardian and guide through the underworld, the place where we face our fears, masks, and our shadow selves. The reptile functions as a catalyst, initiating the experience that will transform us into the beings we aspire to become. It brings the opportunity to cross into new levels in some area of our life, somewhat like crossing from fear to faith.

The teachings continued. Visions, colors, and spiritual energy (vibrations), along with prayer and meditation, all contributed to my spiritual growth and learning. Dreams were very common and in one dream, I clearly saw a large snake. It lay just in front of me and to my right side. The markings were pronounced and its midsection was very thick. It crawled into a nearby rock wall and disappeared. I had no fear at all in this dream. I felt the message was to signify my journey through the underworld.

Spirit often uses dreams to communicate with us. Around this time, I had been doing healings on a man who had been experiencing vision problems. He lived in the western part of the country, so we never met for an in-person session. He was aware of my prayers for him and knew that I followed many Native American ways during my ceremonies. I always began by reading his aura and balancing his chakras. Typically, orange and red would show up. I then prayed for God's healing. His totem, the bear, was employed and I continued my ceremonies by playing my flute and drum. One day, while facing west in his direction, I applied the colors indigo, violet, and red for his healing. I extended my hand to the west. I felt a surge of strong, healing energy as the colors flew from my hand and into the woods.

Two days later, he called me and described a dream he had. In the dream, he was in the center of a circle and Indians were dancing around him. They were singing and calling out, "Bear, bear, bear." He could also hear flute music. How wonderful! Spirit used his dream to communicate that his healing was at hand. The color healing was very effective in improving his vision. I gave thanks to our Creator for this powerful healing.

I saw orbs changing colors as they opened and closed like the petals of a flower. Once, I had a vision of being in a cave or chamber where the walls were made of flaky, red clay. I realized this was not a cave, but a womb, and I was experiencing birth into the physical world.

Frogs, fish, and turtles are frequent visitors, and I see them all over our property. What I didn't expect to see was black scorpions. I had seen very few in the past but now, they seemed to show up everywhere. This was an obvious message, and I needed to pay close attention. I researched the scorpion and learned that they were telling me to watch my temper, which has been an issue with me from time to time. Spirit warned me that it was necessary to control it if things were to go smoothly. I took this to heart and work vigilantly to control anger as it arises.

More visions of faces appeared to me as the days passed. Several were what I thought to be men, but could not be sure, and one was of another Indian woman. This woman was also standing beside a tupa wearing a buckskin dress. Her hair hung in braids down each side of her head and she wore beads around her neck. Their identities have not been revealed to me, but it is certain that they will be when the time is right.

Coming from the Sacred Circle one morning, I looked back at my path and saw red-colored footprints. They were obviously my footprints, but why were they there? It didn't take long to figure out that this was a message to me to better manage my behavior. Our words and actions leave impressions. Spirit wanted me to leave only good impressions that are beneficial to myself and others.

In an early morning ceremony at the Sacred Circle, I took a new stone and placed it as the east marker. The stone that had been the east marker was placed as the north marker. I now had stones at each cardinal direction. I stepped back to check the arrangement of stones. What happened next is truly unbelievable! The spiritual light to the east became so large and bright that it completely blocked out the rising sun. There were countless orbs of various colors floating around me, including a large, red orb and a bright-blue orb in the shape of a perfect circle. The bright-blue orb was flashing and emitting a powerful energy. Orbs were everywhere. Some were in the trees, some were on the ground, and others seemed to soar into the sky. A few seemed so close that I could reach out and touch them. The large, red orb was at a distance, in front of a tree branch. I could actually see the tree branch through the light of the orb. My knees became weak and I found it difficult to stand. This was by far the most spectacular and powerful spiritual experience I have ever had! The vision faded and I gave a very heartfelt prayer of gratefulness and thanks. I collected myself and started walking back to the house. As I walked, I considered that this vision was a powerful teaching on the awesome power of color and that color was a gift from God to be used for His good.

I received an instruction one day that has been very helpful to me in my learning. I tend to be too critical of myself at times. I think we all have that tendency. To remedy this, Spirit sent a vision of an arrow pointing up and one pointing down. When the arrow pointed up, I was being too hard on myself.

When it pointed down, it meant that I had done enough and could rest in the fact that my efforts had been sufficient.

Ax advised me to be alert for the gift of a special stone. It would be black, blue, and indigo. It would have ridges that resemble those of a diamond. He said I would find it as I walk. The Muskogee/Creek Indians believed rocks possess special properties, especially crystals. They called crystals "sabria" and considered them to be good medicine and treated them with great respect.

Several days later, a red-tailed hawk began calling in a loud and rather urgent tone. It flew low over my head and went in the direction of the Sacred Circle. Then, a woodpecker began tapping out his message loud and clear. I went into the house for my flute and drum. As I approached the ceremony site, the birds were still calling and I was seeing orbs. It was time to look for the stone. I felt my steps were guided and I was being drawn to a certain area. There were many stones on the ground but none of them were the sabria stone. After a few minutes, my attention was drawn to a stone that was lying in the wash area of the stream. It was about two and a half inches long and one and a half inches wide. Streaks of black ran the length of the stone and tiny bits of crystals sparkled with light. When I picked it up, strong energy radiated into my hand and up my arm. This was it. This was the gift from Ax, and it would be a powerful tool in my spiritual walk.

My spiritual stone became a part of my daily ceremonies. It would get warm and give off light and color as I held it in my hand. Colored orbs would emerge from the stone, float over the area, and sometimes fade away. Other times they would remain for the entire ceremony.

My lessons have prepared a path for my continuous spiritual journey. All the steps to this point have been to bring me closer to the Divine and to learn the lessons of forgiveness and love. My lessons are in no way complete. Life is a learning process, and I feel my lessons will be ongoing throughout my spiritual journey. It is, however, time to practice these lessons.

Choosing a spiritual path brings incredible growth and joy. The physical, mental, and emotional areas of an individual become equally balanced and learning becomes a welcome need.

As stated earlier, communication with our guides and angels on a daily basis is essential. This is one way we communicate with God. Remember, we are here in the physical world for learning life lessons. If it doesn't challenge you, it won't change you.

Let's move forward and look at healing with color. I have been doing in-person and distance healing for several years now. Each ceremony has music, prayer, and Spirit-guided direction for good and only good. Nature, totems, and Native Americans also play a huge part in healings. Shamans who have passed over surround me and also provide support during the ceremonies. They appear to me as colored orbs with them all being the same color. However, the color will change with each ceremony.

Practice has taught me to refine my healing ceremonies. Each one has four parts. I lead with prayer and identify the individual and the condition to be healed. I then balance the chakras and apply the color given by Spirit. The chakras are then rebalanced and I conclude with prayers of thanksgiving.

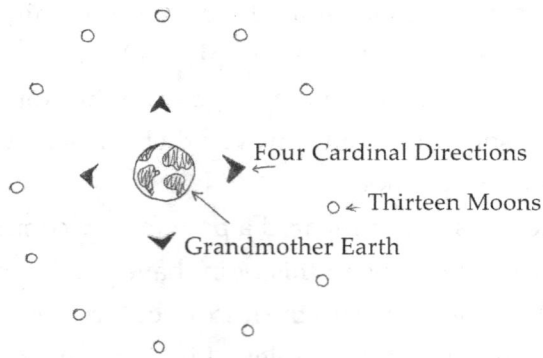

Note: During Healing, Shaman Circle
The Healing Shamans vary from twelve to twenty six

My initiation as a Native American shaman was a major step forward on my spiritual path. The initiation is discussed in more detail in Chapter 7. One week after the initiation, I had another powerful experience. I awoke from sleep about 3:00 a.m. There were white lights all around my bedroom. A few minutes later, my body began to shake with spiritual energy. At the same time, I heard the words, "You are a healer. Why don't you heal others?" My thoughts turned to a young man who was in need of emotional healing. The next morning, Billie and I were walking to the Sacred Circle to pray for the young man. A red-tailed hawk was calling. As we approached the site, many red and teal orbs appeared. Billie gave a stone and cardinal feather as an offering, and we began to pray. Later that day, I offered additional prayers for the young man. I took two bracelets and a special stone for purification and empowerment to the site. During this ceremony, there were orbs like the ones that appeared earlier in the morning ceremony. I asked God to replace the young man's anger and lack of self-confidence with faith and confidence. I asked for him to become fearless. The bracelets and stone warmed in my hand, and I knew that the prayers made their way to our Creator. I gave thanks for the healing and returned to the house. The feather, bracelets, and stone were given to the individual as part of his healing. Healings for him went on for seven weeks. I was given the colors green, bright blue, and white to apply for the relief of his anxieties. During this time, this vision below appeared several times.

Very early morning; awoke to seeing bright white light. Then experienced strong vibrations in my entire body.

Words came to me:
"You are a healer, why don't you heal others?"

Vision:

|— — —|

|— — — — —|

Heal what is broken

Lee Hillberg

    I started taking nature walks after my daily ceremonies. After several trips down the same path, I named it the spiritual trail. I have enjoyed my time on the trail. It brings me peace and joy each time I walk it.

14. Connecting with Spirit

Having a strong connection to Spirit is a blessing beyond compare. I am filled with awe, peace, comfort, and love!

In this writing, I have described experiences from my early years to today. All of them have been a journey of many lessons and learnings. It is my firm belief that we are all here in the physical world to learn and gain knowledge beneficial to our spiritual growth. As our soul grows, we become closer to the divine.

I feel that most of my time here in this life was to prepare me for what I do today. It has allowed me to grow in love, understanding, and forgiveness. The greater your contact with Spirit, the more frequent and stronger these all become.

The stronger you become in faith, the more you will be able to recognize the presence and communications of Spirit and the Creator. We can then help others to do the same. Just as I stated before, everyone has their own method of connecting with Spirit. Is everything we encounter a sign or message from Spirit? No. However, all things have meanings and importance. How do we know when we have received a special message? Experience is key. You will learn to recognize things that are unusual or out of the ordinary. I find that Spirit will send a message three times and in various ways to ensure that I receive it. Our spiritual guides want us to be happy and to achieve our life goals. They are our cheerleaders. They will help only when we ask them to, as this is our journey and ours alone.

There have been so many spiritual encounters in my life. Some have been extraordinary; some have been less so, but they have all been meaningful.

I was doing healing on a woman in her midfifties who suffered from both emotional and physical maladies. Over the course of three years, I had done both in-person and distance healing on her. This particular time was an in-person healing. We were at the ceremonial circle on our property. In addition to color healing, I was also passing messages from Spirit to her. She wanted to connect with her father on the other side. He had passed a few years earlier. While I assured her that he was with her and supported her at all times, she wanted positive proof that he was a part of this ceremony. So, I suggested a different approach from that we had been taking. I told her to spend an extended amount of time, about an hour, and focus on a special color. This color would be representative of her father. She was not to tell anyone the color she had chosen until after the reading. We adjourned and she went off to meditate and focus on her color. When we met again an hour later at the ceremonial circle, she said she was ready to continue. Her totem, the owl, was placed nearby, and we were both seated, facing each other. We began with prayer, then I asked her to once again focus on the color she had chosen for her father. I drew a circle with her father's name on a piece of white paper and placed it on the ground between us. A minute or two passed when I placed my index finger on his name. The color green appeared to me. I said, "Your father is here. The color is green." She looked at me with tears in her eyes and confirmed that green was indeed the color she had chosen. We then went forward with the healing and I passed the messages from Spirit to her. It is interesting to note that I had not asked Spirit to come in this way before. Spirit directed me to proceed in this fashion due to her need for confirmation. This was very moving and meaningful to her.

Another healing involved a man I met through my interest in Native Americans and Native American artifacts. He was active at powwows and other such activities. Tragically, his brother had recently been shot and killed, and he was still grieving his loss. Billie and I invited him and his wife to our house for lunch and further discussions. I asked if I could hold a prayer ceremony for him at the ceremonial circle. I indicated that I felt it would be a time of healing for him and for his deceased brother. He agreed, and the next morning, I went to the Sacred Circle with him on my list of those needing Spirit's help. I began in my usual way, then proceeded with prayers for the brothers. I drew a circle on the paper and wrote his brother's name on it. Again, I laid the paper on the ground in the center of the site and placed my finger on his name. Immediately, the color orange appeared along with the intuitive message, "He is joyful and happy. Please pass this message to his brother." After the ceremony, I did just as I was asked by Spirit. I called the brother and gave him the message. Understandably, he was very quiet, but I could tell that the news moved him. He did convey that he was very grateful for the news.

In about an hour, he called back. He had regained his composure and wanted to thank me for the message. We talked a few minutes about recent experiences that he, himself, had regarding animals and snakes. I told him that these were no doubt messages from his brother. He shared, with obvious excitement, that he always wore his hair long and always wore a turban. However, he very seldom wore colorful turbans. This particular day he had chosen to wear an orange one. When I called and told him that orange was the color I had seen in my spiritual connection with his brother, he was overcome with emotion. He said he couldn't respond immediately but this message definitely gave him comfort at a very difficult time.

Through my connection with Native American culture, I sometimes receive requests for presentations and speaking engagements. One special call came from the relative of a woman who had recently passed over. I was to perform Indian prayers at her memorial service. She was part Cherokee Indian, and the family wanted her heritage included in the memorial services. I was happy to be a part of the celebration of her life and heritage. The next morning, I said a prayer for the deceased woman and asked Spirit for guidance with the prayers I was to contribute at the service. Three orbs appeared. The center orb was bright blue and the other two were red and yellow. I asked Spirit if the center blue orb was the woman who had crossed over. Yes, it was. I later called her family, telling them what I had seen. From our conversation, I knew that the woman's parents had crossed over years ago. I knew then that the yellow and red orbs were her mother and father, who were there supporting her in her transition.

The memorial service was the following day. Billie and I made the two-hour trip to North Georgia, taking printed copies of the prayers I would be offering and a hawk feather with me. I felt that the hawk was her totem and wanted to include it in the service. I also wanted to give each of her family members a copy of the prayers and a feather.

Upon arriving at the service, I met with the family. As we were talking, I saw a bright-blue orb over our heads. A hawk was also calling out at the same time. I told the family what was happening. The family felt comforted in knowing that their loved one was still there with them, showering them with her love and support.

Over the next several months, this woman's spirit sent several messages to her family through me. Each time, I called the family and conveyed her communication, helping them to heal in the transition.

Confirmation

In my spiritual journey, I have had a broad array of experiences, teachings, and other spiritual encounters. I have enjoyed learning more about the Native American way, how to heal with color, and clairvoyant experiences and visions. Each step has had a tremendous impact on my life. God and Spirit have shown me nothing but love and support throughout my walk, and I am honored for the opportunities they have given me.

It is only natural that I questioned myself at times, wondering, *Did I get this right?* Most of the time, this doubt surfaced when I was performing healings or when I received messages for others. Early on, I started asking for confirmation by requesting that a certain color appear. I tried to limit the confirmation to a yes or no answer. For example, I would say, "If I am right, show red," or "If I am wrong, show green." I don't believe that Spirit is troubled by our questions. As I have grown in Spirit, I find that I need confirmation less often. There are still times when I do not receive a clear vision or answer. When this happens, I usually think about my question and restate it in another way. Using color to guide the confirmations has been very helpful to me in my growth and confidence as a healer.

Orbs and Colors

My journey has been blessed with many wonderful learning experiences. I have the privilege of seeing colors and orbs, receiving spiritual messages, performing healings, and spreading love and forgiveness. This sketch is an example of those messages.

The appearance of orbs has been a big part of my experience. The Webster dictionary describes orbs as "(1) any of the concentric spheres in old astronomy surrounding the earth and carrying the celestial bodies in their revolutions. (2) Something circular. And (3) to form into a disc."

Lee Hillberg

Heart-shaped orbs
First colors blue/green;
Color changed to red
Indian brothers and sisters: "Love"
Vision: Sacred-circle orbs

I see orbs as circles of light, or energy forms that appear in many ways. They are usually a round, but not perfect, circle. However, they have appeared as square or rectangular. They can be a single color or multicolored. They seem to be flexible and move in many directions and at various speeds. Physical barriers do not exist for them, as they can move in and out of any object as easily as through the air. The movement and color of the orbs are significant in that they communicate different messages.

Colored orbs are a huge part of my healing ceremonies. For me, they are a way of identifying spirits of family members or friends of the individual needing healing. Once identified, the spirit orb will always appear as the same color in subsequent healings. This is very beneficial when communicating with Spirit and deciphering the messages. The orbs come from my hands, stones, feathers, wood, etc. Mother, my grandmother, attends all of my ceremonies for support and is always the color purple.

One Man's Spiritual Journey to Healing with Color Energy

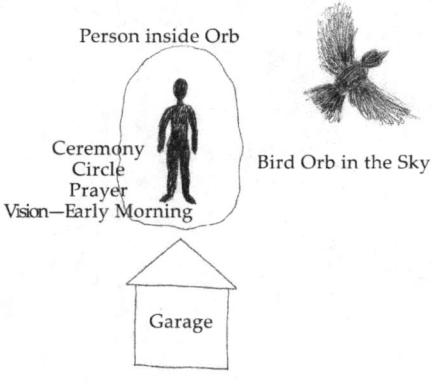

Elephant
Message: Power,
Strength & Royalty

Ram's Head
Message: Seeking
New Beginnings

Lee Hillberg

Purple Flower

Orbs Dancing
"Joy, Be Happy"

Meditation

Each night, I meditate in my bedroom before going to sleep. I light a candle, say prayers, and engage in quiet thought. However, I am never alone during my meditation. Orbs of my family members fill the room, dancing from place to place. Some will even come to rest in the palm of my hand. It is an endearing display of love and support that I anticipate with great joy.

One night, two years ago, I received a strong message from my spirit family. The top half of the bedroom wall turned black. I knew black was a protective color so I knew this message was a warning. Apparently, a person whom I had met in a spiritual workshop was trying to discredit my reputation. Later, a friend confirmed that the individual had, in fact, been talking about me in an attempt to demean my abilities as a healer. I was grateful for the warning.

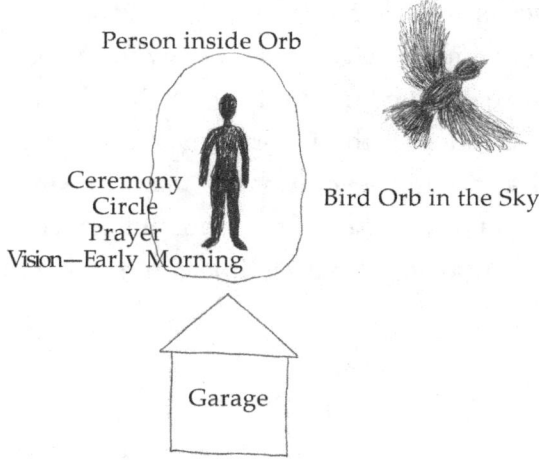

Challenge

There was one experience that challenged me beyond any other. It elicited a broad range of feelings that affected my relationships and personal encounters before it was resolved. I recognize it now as a path to healing and change for myself and the others involved. As I stated earlier, "If it doesn't challenge you, it doesn't change you." Well, this experience did both.

Two people, other than myself, were the principals in this situation. A man and a woman. They had known each other for a number of years. Their relationship had been fairly distant as they both followed their own life journey. As fate would have it, they reconnected in their fifties and began seeing each other regularly. Their jobs, travel, and relocation threw them curve balls that caused trouble in the relationship. Family members also played a part in the rough spots.

I became involved after being introduced at a family gathering. The need to intercede spiritually was strong. I began praying several times a week for healing and direction. I also asked Spirit to advise me on how to move forward with any issues that may arise. Spirit responded, "Trust your intuition."

A few weeks later, I received a very strong message from Spirit during my morning ceremony. I saw the image of a person. I couldn't make out the face but believed it to be the man in the relationship. Suddenly, the mental image of a hand appeared and pointed at the midsection of the man. I heard, intuitively, that this man was "weak here," meaning that he required healing that would be necessary for a lifetime commitment between the two people.

Sacred Circle
Mid-Morning
Vision-Prayer

Message Delivered with
Stronger Spirit Energy

Anxiety grew among us as I tried to express my concerns about the messages from Spirit. I remained persistent in prayer, using yellow, red, indigo, and citrine as provided by Spirit. I sent forward only the messages conveyed by Spirit. The totems of both of them were placed at the site as well. Her totem was the owl, and his was the snake. My ceremonies for healing and guidance for all involved, including myself, went on for several months. Feedback said that I should accept things as they were. Everyone was unhappy with me, but Spirit advised, "Don't let that bother you, because the couple cannot see clearly at this time."

Three months later, neither party is getting it. Information was being withheld by both. I continued prayers and healings. Spirit sent a message: "Beware of things that are not genuine."

A few days later, I had another experience. I was about to enter the Sacred Circle for my morning ceremonies when I noticed a lot of blue-jay feathers. They were in a tree and all over the ground around the Sacred Circle. It appeared the blue jay had been killed and eaten by another bird high in the tree. Intuition told me that an owl had made a meal of the blue jay. I found that interesting since the totem of the woman of the couple happened to be an owl. The message I received from my spirit guide was that the woman should beware. He said, "Someone is trying to deceive you. Attack your fears courageously. Assess your main gifts and talent and finish this project." I felt the urgency to relay this information to the woman of the relationship. I asked Spirit to show me the color green for confirmation that I had the message correct and that I should pass it on. Boom! Green immediately covered my entire right hand. That was clear enough. I then asked if she would be receptive to the message. If so, show me red. Bingo! A large, red orb appeared in my hand. Given the history and delicacy of this situation, I asked Spirit to help me arrange the meeting and deliver the message. A violet orb appeared in confirmation of my request. I arranged the meeting and presented Spirit's message regarding the blue jay and the owl.

Approximately one month later, another spiritual message came my way concerning this relationship. I was sitting on a stump at the Sacred Circle when I felt something to my right side. I peered over my right shoulder and there, three to four feet from me, sat the biggest opossum I had ever seen! It didn't seem the least bit afraid of me. It turned slowly and walked into the woods. After it left, I moved to another location in the circle and continued my prayers. To my surprise, another opossum came out into the open. This one was smaller than the first. It lingered for a few minutes and finally exited via the path of the first opossum. Now, this was unusual. One opossum visiting was odd enough. But two of them was unheard of. Still, I maintained a state of solemnity and persisted in prayer. I couldn't believe it when I looked up and saw yet another opossum! This one was coming out of the woods and walking straight for me! Before reaching me, it turned and went slightly into the woods. It was still in plain view as it walked all the way around me outside the Sacred Circle.

Sacred Circle

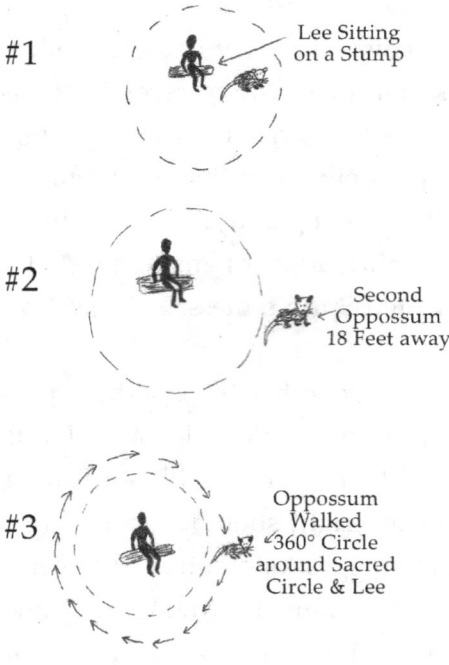

Obviously, this was a message that could not be ignored. Spirit was telling me, "If you are in a tight corner, rely on your instincts. Develop effective tactics, or you will feel you are being misled in some way." The couple's relationship remained difficult, but they were trying to work out their differences. I remained steadfast in the messages I had been receiving and continued to deliver them as I was told by Spirit, even though it caused damage to some of my own relationships.

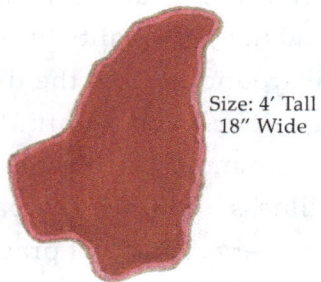

Size: 4' Tall
18" Wide

Message: It has to run its course.

Thankfully, their paths began to clear. The man saw the need for change and received counseling to heal from personal problems. Gradually, both parties began to grow and change in their own areas of need. Messages from Spirit stopped as the relationship grew stronger.

Today, all parties are happy, living in love and balance. All have found the courage to walk fearlessly through this world knowing that it would not have been possible without the spiritual guidance and direction from Spirit. All should rejoice!

Everyone is capable of change. Change is our reason for living on this earth. It brings us to a new level of love and forgiveness which, in turn, brings us closer to the Divine.

Family Experiences

In 2010, Billie's sister suffered serious health issues. The most devastating was Parkinson's disease, a progressive disease that is somewhat manageable, but not curable. As the disease advanced, her sister needed around-the-clock care to fulfill her medical needs and maintain her living capacity.

Through God's guidance and Billie's perseverance, an outstanding facility located in North Georgia became available to her. The care she received there was exemplary. The staff was attentive, loving, and compassionate. She was truly happy there, and her personality blossomed, spreading her love to all those around her. As the disease progressed, living became more difficult and painful for her. She began exhibiting dementia, paranoia, depression, and fear.

Throughout the illness and until she passed, Billie was a constant in her life in every capacity. I prayed for her and her needs daily as well. I asked the universe questions about her life's journey. "Is it time for her to go home yet?" The answer was, "Not at this time, her passing will not be for a while. The way is ready." This, of course, came intuitively and accompanied by many white doves. Prayers for her peace and comfort were always accompanied with high spiritual energy.

We all knew she was nearing the end of her physical life on this earth. Billie asked her mother, who had passed many years ago, about the imminent event, and she responded, "It will be sooner than later."

On the afternoon of November 28, 2012, Billie had just returned from visiting her sister. Later that evening, Billie heard a bird pecking on the windows around the house. Upon inspection, she found that the sound was coming from inside the house. As she walked around the house searching for the source of the pecking, a radio started playing. As it happens, this was a portable AM beach radio that ran on batteries and had not been played in over forty years! It was a keepsake from her late husband and kept as a bookend on a cabinet in the family room. The audio was excellent, with no static at all. Men were heard talking and their voices were as clear as a bell. It was shocking to us, and we quickly realized that this was a message from Spirit.

That night, I had a ceremony in my bedroom to ask Spirit the meaning of the pecking sound and radio playing. I lit a white candle and began meditation. A very clear, large, purple orb appeared on the wall. I asked many questions. "Is she passing over at this time?" The answer was, "No. The sounds were from a spirit close to Billie, letting her know that she will be notified when her sister passes over." I then received another large, purple orb in my hand as a confirmation. This orb was Mother. Purple is her spiritual color.

A month later during my ceremonies at the Sacred Circle, I was praying for Billie's sister. Totems of the red-tailed hawk, great blue heron, and woodpecker stood nearby. There was high spiritual energy with many colored orbs everywhere. The blue orb for peace and comfort and another orange orb for joy appeared. Soon, green, violet, pink, red, and lavender followed. They were there to lend support to her sister and to say that angels were with her. Her passing would be soon.

The last time Billie saw her sister was on January 13, 2013. Just as the spiritual message promised, Billie was notified of her sister's passing. She left this world peacefully on January 14, 2013, well attended by family, angels, and Spirit. Prayers of thanksgiving and gratitude were offered.

The next morning as I stepped outside, a red-tailed hawk was already calling. At the ceremony, there were prayers for the soul that had crossed over and was now at home and at peace. Prayers for the family were offered to provide comfort, enlightenment, compassion, and love. Orbs of white, yellow, blue, violet, and red were present and abundant.

On January 18, I was conducting a ceremony in preparation for the funeral services, the family, and those who were travelling to the service when this orb appeared:

The day of the funeral service, January 19, 2013, Billie and I were leaving for the two-hour drive to the services. We were still in the driveway when a bright-green orb trimmed in red appeared near the ground in front of the car. Spirit was sending us comfort and love.

When we reached the church where the services would be held, Billie and I stopped in a nearby parking lot. We sat quietly and gathered our thoughts. Colors started appearing on the dashboard and on the inside of the car. I looked up and saw colors in the sky. Yellow, green, orange, violet, and purple spirit orbs of family members gathered in the crowd to lend their love and support.

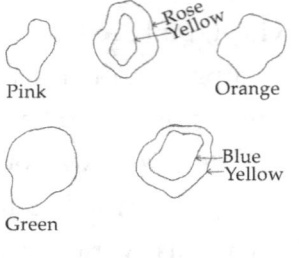

Pink—Love, Purity, Comfort
Orbs Family

Ironically, when Billie's mother passed years ago, she lay in state on the birthday of the sister we were here to celebrate. Today, January 19, was their mother's birthday.

While praying, I had a vision and received several messages from Spirit to heal the family members. A huge, pink spirit orb appeared. Pink awakens compassion, love, and purity and is meant to comfort the emotional energies of an individual.

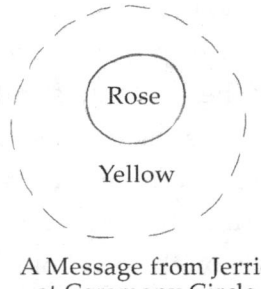

A Message from Jerrie
at Ceremony Circle

Billie's sister was present at her own funeral service, as many souls are. As I indicated earlier, souls enter a period of review after they enter into the spiritual realm. They are not available and cannot be contacted while in their review. Billie's sister had indeed achieved her life's goals because her review was short. Only two or three months passed before she was an active participant in my daily ceremonies!

Crossing Over

Death is the passage, or transition, of a soul from a body on this earth into the spirit world. At death, the soul immediately leaves the body and is met by angels, family, and friends who have gone before them. We miss our loved ones when they pass, but once they pass, they are home! Everyone returns home . . . to be with God in Heaven.

For a short period, the soul stays close to the physical world. The soul can see its earthly body and most attend their own funeral before passing to the heavenly realm. However, it is not so much about the body as it about the soul and what was learned in this incarnation. Once passing, the soul enters a period of review, or an account, of the earthly life. Think of the review process like that of going through customs or immigration. There are certain checkpoints, "loving" checkpoints. Did you learn to love? Did you accomplish in this lifetime what you failed to accomplish in previous lifetimes? This is not a horrible experience, as the soul longs to know if the goals of their lifetime on earth were met. The soul feels joy when the learning or lessons were accomplished. It feels wrath from the poor choices made during that lifetime. The amount of time spent in review depends on the level of success the individual had in attaining his or her goals. The better life one leads, the quicker the review is accomplished.

Since I began healing with color, I have had some very strong spiritual contact from those who have passed and are in the transition period. There have been many times when I was notified that a soul was near death and would soon cross over. Usually, I would receive a pure-white color in connection with prayer for that person. After passing, I would attempt to contact them and ask for a color to be associated with their spirit. When and if they do come through and show as a color, they are usually accompanied by family members or friends that have passed before them. I am sometimes surprised by the large number of spirits who accompany those in transition.

Learnings

I would like to take a look at my journey thus far. Starting in the early years in the Black Hills of South Dakota and progressing to this point in my life, I realize that we all come to this life to learn lessons that will bring us closer to the divine. Our life lessons are known before our birth but forgotten after birth.

We all question, "Why am I here? What am I here to learn?" Look at the problems in your life. Conflicts, tragedies, anything that does not bring joy and happiness to your life is a lesson you are here to learn.

All things are connected. Our life experiences make us who we are.

There are thousands of lessons, and we each have our own. We can each look at our lives in a realistic, balanced way and change that which prevents total love. God gives us many opportunities to come back to earth (earth school) and make amends for the hurt we may have caused in other's lives.

My lessons started in the Black Hills. Cowboys, Indians, Dust Bowl, poverty, séances, religion, dysfunctional family relationships, and hard work on the farm and school—all of these were a part of my formative years. But with all of this came hope, faith, and the belief that my life had meaning and purpose. I always believed that angels were in my path and that those angels came in many different forms, spiritual and human. I also believed that we, ourselves, could serve as angels in the lives of others.

Each of us has a very large support system in our family, friends, and God's total being. Spiritual guides and nature are just two of the vast array of those devoted to our love and care.

My experiences in the air force, business, family, and daily living were preparing me for this journey, my spiritual walk. I have grown in faith and learned much about God, our Creator. I have learned that there is only one God and that all religions are valid. Every lifetime has meaning and a purpose and there is a reason for everything you experience here on earth. Most importantly, I have learned that every person is a special and deeply, unconditionally loved soul. It is imperative that we know and believe this. If you don't, you cannot give love nor can you receive love.

I will say that the two most powerful lessons I have learned in this lifetime are forgiveness and love.

God wants us to live by these simple truths:
- Love yourself
- Love one another
- Be true to your word
- Don't try to conquer that which does not belong to you
- Live by ethical standards
- Portray to the world love

God has blessed me with a wonderful journey and my lessons and learning are ongoing. From the early years to now, I have been given a remarkable life. With the guidance of Spirit, I look forward to the opportunity to continue on this path and spread the gift I have been given of God's healing power with colors.

God's Greatest Gifts Are Love and Forgiveness

Love

    In our culture, the definition of love varies according to the giver and receiver.

    We all focus deeply upon creating love. It is the most desired among all things. So why is it so elusive for many?

    Love begins within the self. The expression, "If you can't love yourself, you can't love anyone else," is commonplace.

    Loving one's self means having the courage to listen to the heart's emotional messages and spiritual directions.

    Self-love means caring for ourselves enough to forgive ourselves and the people in our past who have caused us harm. Our wounds do not hurt the people who hurt us, they only hurt us.

    Forgiveness is an essential spiritual act that must occur in order to open oneself fully to the healing power of love. Healing is possible through acts of forgiveness.

    Take a look at all aspects of yourself and begin to transform the negative into positive.

    Remove all conditions. Know who you are and love it. Yes, even the negative part of your consciousness, because it needs the greatest change.

    As you begin to see yourself more lovingly, you will attract those who would love you unconditionally.

    Awake each day pleased with who you are.

Forgiveness

What is forgiveness?

Generally, forgiveness is a decision to let go of resentment and thoughts of revenge. Forgiveness is one of the most compassionate actions one can take. It's a gift you give yourself.

Most all of us have been impacted by negative experiences. These unhealed wounds can keep us living in the past and are harmful to our mental and physical health.

Self-love means forgiving ourselves and caring for ourselves enough to forgive people in our past. Wounds do not hurt the people who hurt us, they only hurt us.

Perhaps today, take a few moments to examine that huge weight of undesirable emotions and leave them behind once and for all.

To truly learn your life lessons, you also have to be willing to let go of your negative emotions. Nothing is served by stubbornly clinging to a negative perspective. Decide to embrace, forgive, and release.

Be free. Just let go of all your resentment and anger. The benefits are healthier relationships, peace, kindness, less stress, and greater happiness, to name a few.

Be free . . . forgive . . . you are worth your own redemption.

Native American Medicine Wheel

In Native American society, the Medicine Wheel represents harmony and connections and is considered a major symbol of peaceful interaction among all living beings on Earth. The Medicine Wheel is sometimes referred to as the Sacred Hoop. Its focus is on the balance of all things.

Medicine equals vital power or force that is inherent in nature itself and to the personal power within one's self to become more whole/complete.

The Medicine Wheel represents the sacred circle of life, its four directions, and the elements. Animal totems serve as guardians of each of the directions. The four animals commonly represented in this role are the bear, the buffalo, the eagle, and the mouse. However, there are no fast rules about which animals represent the cardinal directions of the Medicine Wheel. Most native people have different animal totems and meanings of the directions, encouraging us in choosing our own. Each direction of the wheel offers its own lessons, color, and animal spirit guides.

Medicine Wheel Elements and Directions

- Four Elements
    - Air, Water, Fire, Earth
- Four Directions
    - North, East, South, West
- Seven Directions
    - North, East, South, West, Sky (Great Spirit), Mother Earth, Center (Self)
- Four Sacred Colors
    - Red, Yellow, Black, White
- Four symbolic races are all part of the same human family

- Four aspects of nature
    Mental, Physical, Emotional, Spiritual

Muskogee Nation—Creek Tribe Seven Sacred Directions

South
- We came upon this planet from the South
- Color is white: the new fallen snow with no tracks; the path is clear
- The animal in charge of this direction is the egret
- From the South, all other directions are open to us

West
- End of each day, we say our thanks for we all are grateful for experiences both good and bad; we are grateful for these necessary teachings
- Color is black
- The animal in charge is the spotted eagle
- From the West, we receive all waters, thunder beings (black thunderclouds), and lightning
- Direction of the great mystery

North
- Direction of purifying winds; healing of mind, body, and soul
- Color is red: like the pipe used when communicating with God; like the color of our blood
- The animal in charge is the bald eagle

East
- Direction of enlightenment, knowledge, and wisdom
- Color is yellow
- Grandparents come to you, walk to the East to meet them; have a heart-to-heart talk, gain knowledge, how to use this knowledge when it's time in a good way

All Living Things
- The circle around YOU (Self in center)
- Color for this direction is the rainbow
- Completeness of beauty

Grandmother Earth
- Supports all living things
- The source is to sustain all life, in all life forms
- Color of this direction is green

The One Above
- The Great Spirit
- All energy, all knowledge, all love, all forgiveness, and much, much more
- There are no limits, no defects
- Complete freedom out of love
- Color is blue like the sky
- Speak directly to God; be grateful

Special Messages

"Do Not Stand at My Grave and Weep"
Mary Elizabeth Frye, 1932

Do not stand at my grave and weep
I am not there. I do not sleep.
I am a thousand winds that blow.
I am the diamond glints on snow.
I am the sunlight on ripened grain.
I am the gentle autumn rain.
When you awaken in the morning's hush
I am the swift uplifting rush
Of quiet birds in circled flight.
I am the soft stars that shine at night.
Do not stand at my grave and cry;
I am not there. I did not die.

"An Indian Prayer"
Lakota Chief Yellow Lark, 1887

Oh, Great Spirit,
whose voice I hear in the winds
and whose breath gives life to all the world, hear me.
I am small and weak.
I need your strength and wisdom.

Let me walk in beauty and make my eyes
ever behold the red and purple sunset.
Make my hands respect the things you have made
and my ears sharp to hear your voice.
Make me wise so that I may understand
the things you have taught my people.
Let me learn the lessons you have hidden
in every leaf and rock.

I seek strength, not to be superior to my brother,
but to fight my greatest enemy - myself.
Make me always ready to come to you
with clean hands and straight eyes,
so when life fades, as the fading sunset,
my spirit will come to you
without shame.

Bibliography

Andrews, Ted. *Animal-Speak: The Spiritual & Magical Powers of Creatures Great & Small*. St. Paul: Llewellyn Publications, 1993.

Andrews, Ted. *Animal-Wise: The Spirit Language and Signs of Nature*. Jackson, TN: Dragonhawk Pub, 1999.

Andrews, Ted. *How to Heal with Color*. St. Paul: Llewellyn Publications, 1992.

Andrews, Ted. *How to See and Read the Aura*. St. Paul: Llewelly Publications, 1991.

Andrews, Ted. *Nature-Speak: Signs, Omens & Messages in Nature*. Jackson, TN: Dragonhawk Pub, 2004.

Shepard, Carter and Carolyn Cummings. *What they want you to know! Messages from Beyond the Grave*. Atlanta: Cumming Press, 2007.

"Dust Bowl." *Wikipedia*. Accessed August 31, 2016. https://en.wikipedia.org/wiki/DustBowl.

Farmer, Stephen. *Animal Spirit Guides: An Easy-to-Use Handbook for Identifying and Understanding Your Power Animals and Animal Spirit Helpers*. Carlsbad, CA: Hay House, 2006.

"Golden History." *Lead Area Chamber of Commerce*. Accessed August 31, 2016. http://www.leadmethere.org/history/.

Heart, Bear and Molly Larkin. *The Wind Is My Mother: The Life and Teachings of a Native American Shaman*. New York: Clarkson Potter, 1996.

"Lockheed EC-121 Warning Star." *Wikipedia*. Accessed August 31, 2016. https://en.wikipedia.org/wiki/Lockheed_EC-121_Warning_Star.

"Rodeo." *Days of '76*. Accessed August 31, 2016. http://daysof76.com/rodeo.

"South Dakota Legends: Rough & Tumble Deadwood." *Legends of America*. Accessed August 31, 2016. http://www.legendsofamerica.com/sd-deadwood.html.

Webster, Richard. *Spirit Guides & Angel Guardians: Contact Your Invisible Helpers*. St. Paul: Llewellyn Publications, 1998.

"When Weather Changes, Grasshopper Turns Locust." *The New York Times*. Accessed August 31, 2016. http://www.nytimes.com/2013/04/09/science/when-weather-changes-grasshopper-turns-locust.html?r=0.

About the Author

Lee Hillberg was born and raised in the Black Hills of South Dakota. After high school, he attended advanced-study programs at Dakota Wesleyan University, University of Chicago, and Duke University.

He spent four years in the US Air Force in national defense. Later, he established himself in the corporate world with a Fortune 500 company specializing in national security and commercial electronics. He travelled worldwide in this position and retired as a vice president in 1996.

Lee has always had a keen interest in nature, Native Americans, and spirituality. As a naturalist, he has a strong love for all of nature. As a Native American historian, he occasionally gives lectures on their culture at local venues.

He has been a student of metaphysics and spirituality for a number of years and is now an ordained minister.

He lectures and conducts energy healing and spirituality workshops.

Lee now lives in a rural area of Georgia, enjoying his daily nature walks.

www.ingramcontent.com/pod-product-compliance
Lightning Source LLC
Chambersburg PA
CBHW070137080526
44586CB00015B/1736